Finding Your Chicago Irish

Sharon Shea Bossard

First Edition

LAKE CLAREMONT PRESS
www.lakeclaremont.com
Chicago

Finding Your Chicago Irish
Sharon Shea Bossard

Published July 2008 by:

P.O. Box 711
Chicago, IL 60690-0711
lcp@lakeclaremont.com

Copyright © 2008 by Sharon Shea Bossard

Publisher's Cataloging-In-Publication Data
(Prepared by The Donohue Group, Inc.)

Bossard, Sharon Shea.
Finding your Chicago Irish / Sharon Shea Bossard. – 1st ed.

p. : ill. ; cm.

Includes bibliographical references and index.
ISBN: 978-1-893121-37-9

1. Irish Americans–Illinois–Chicago–Social life and customs–Guidebooks. 2. Cookery, Irish. 3. Chicago (Ill.)–Guidebooks. I. Title.

F548.18 .B67 2008
917.73/110443   2008920821

11 10 09 08   10 9 8 7 6 5 4 3 2 1

To my grandparents, Michael Healy and Sarah Beirne from
County Roscommon and Michael Shea and Bridget Murphy from
County Kerry, for the gift of this country.

To my wonderful husband, Phil, for his time, energy, ideas, valuable
assistance, countless miles, and extraordinary adventures.

Contents

Chapter 10: Canines 157

Irish Dog Breeds

Chapter 11: Citizenship and Genealogy 161

Irish Citizenship

By Birth, Application, or Descent
Documents Relating to Your Grandparent, Parent, and the Applicant

Genealogy: The Search!

Getting Started: The Four Ws
Collecting Paperwork
Libraries and Other Resources
Resources in Ireland
Genealogy by Genetics

Chapter 12: Recipes 175

Irish Breads and Cakes
Irish Meat and Potatoes
Irish Coffee

Foreword

It's finally been written—a guide, a GPS of sorts, for everything Irish in Chicago. If you're thinking it's a pub book or a collection of limericks, think again. Sure, you'll find pubs listed in this book, but you'll be directed to the pubs where true Irish musicians perform the traditional Irish music. There are tips to impress the pub crowd, but this book goes beyond all the paddywhackery of the jokes and the offensive reference to the drink and raises the bar; this book represents the heart and soul of Irish heritage and culture in Chicago.

Locate Chicago's Irish theater, film, educational opportunities, dance, music, heritage centers, sports, parades, organizations, clubs, St. Patrick's Day activities, and performers. Discover the Irish language. Learn about the radio and TV stations that cater to Chicago's Irish and Irish American community. Identify your favorite specialty stores that stock all things Irish. Get cozy with an Irish newspaper, a brisk cup of Irish tea, and delicious homemade soda bread right from your oven—family recipes are included. Longing for a faithful companion? Familiarize yourself with Irish dog breeds listed herein. And for those looking to indulge in a worthwhile endeavor, take a gander at the genealogy section—turn dates into names and forgotten people into family. Explore the possibility of becoming an Irish citizen.

Tuck this book into your backpack, briefcase, saddlebag, or glove box. Consider storing an extra copy on the table next to your bed or easy chair. Keep it handy, because this is your field guide—a comprehensive, informative, and fun book for the tourist in all of us.

Sláinte! And enjoy the journey!

Introduction

When the publisher asked me to write a book titled *Finding Your Chicago Irish*, my initial thought was a genealogy book—a roadmap of sorts. After all, I had located my grandparents' elusive cottages in Ireland, so I did know something about the journey. But the publisher, Sharon Woodhouse, had a different idea of what this book should be. She envisioned a guide outlining the variety of opportunities available to all those interested in Chicago's Irish community. Delighted with this new possibility, I was energized to begin.

Chicago is my hometown. My grandparents Sarah Beirne and Michael Healy began their lives together in this city, arriving from County Roscommon in 1903. My father, Mike Shea, the seventh son of poor Irish immigrants, made his way from Omaha to Chicago in 1922, finding work in the stockyards. Those were hard times for the Irish and Irish Americans, but their strong sense of ethnic pride and rural tradition banded them together in neighborhoods, pubs, and political arenas of the city.

Neighborhoods such as Mt. Greenwood, Beverly, Lakeview, Jefferson Park, and Edison Park found the Irish settling in, raising families, building parishes, and contributing their talents to help shape this great city. They created clubs and organizations where the traditions and values of a culture steeped in history could thrive.

Parades, pubs, and drinking songs all contribute to the limited view of what it means to be Irish—a stereotypical one at best, because there is more to the spectrum—more than just shamrocks and green beer.

There are Chicago's immigrant Irish who fled Ireland in the mid 1950s for the opportunities this city provided, the Irish Americans who speak of their Irish roots with pride, revealing what it truly means to be Irish in this city, identifying the heartbeat—the pulse.

Late evenings found my husband and me nursing many a pint while listening to traditional Irish music sessions in the old pubs throughout the city. Soft, woeful sounds of the uilleann pipes, lively jigs from the fiddles, polka rhythms floating from button accordions, and the brushed taps of the bodhrán introduced us to a sort of music we'd never heard before in Chicago. Like some well-guarded secret, these extraordinary music sessions go on all over the city on any given afternoon and evening with very little advertisement or fanfare.

We racked up the miles traveling to the Irish American Heritage Center to participate in their events. Theater, benefits, book signings, library affairs, pub entertainment, Shamrock Club doings—there is no end to the wealth of Irish-themed activities at this remarkable old school building on Knox. And if you're wondering where the Irish hang out, you'll find them here, devoting hours and hours to keeping the place up and running. Dedicated men like Irish-born Ambrose Kelly volunteer their time and talents so that we Irish and Irish Americans have a place to gather and celebrate our heritage.

Gaelic Park in Oak Forest is another treasure trove of Irish events and activities. Spend time in their Carraig Pub and leave thinking you've just passed an evening in one of the old pubs in Ireland; this is where the South Side Irish hang their caps. And don't leave the park without stopping at the Famine Memorial, a grim reminder of why our ancestors fled their homeland.

Spend Sunday afternoon cheering your favorite Gaelic football and hurling teams or, better yet, join in the game; it's great exercise. Give Irish road bowling—one of the oldest sports in Ireland—a whirl. And if it's the boat racing you're after, contact the Currach Club to find out how you can get involved in this thrilling event.

Participate in Chicago's Irish parades, festivals and celebrations. Everyone is welcome; you don't have to be Irish to appreciate the traditions and culture of an ancient land whose history reflects the spirit of America.

I've included a bit of genealogy, for once you've experienced the true music of Ireland, danced the céilí, and shared in the cultural activities throughout Chicago and its suburbs, you might be inspired to investigate your Irish—your link to that small island with its incredible landscapes and ancient castles set alongside modern, bustling cities.

The Irish have an old saying, "Put *nia* into it," nia meaning "splendid nature" or "heart." My hope is that all who read this book appreciate its *nia*, because doing any task with heart becomes a labor of love.

And now it's time to begin celebrating your Irish in Chicago!

Cinema and Theater

Poster from The Quiet Man *movie.*

It's always a treat to be able to view an Irish movie that's not only directed and produced in Ireland but that has an all-Irish cast. So when the movie *The Wind That Shakes the Barley* came to Chicago's Music Box Theatre on Southport Avenue, I was the first in line to purchase a ticket. Winner of the Palme d'Or Award at the 2006 Cannes Film Festival, this movie should be on your must-see list. The dramatic portrayal of working-class life and oppression shaded in dark, fog-on-the-moor colors offers a complicated vision into the political violence of the 1920s. Though difficult to understand at first because of the Irish accents, listen and watch closely; you'll learn a bit of Irish history and you'll be gifted with a view of the *Ould Sod*. Ireland itself plays a major role in the cinema. The Emerald Isle holds a special allure, not only for its scenic beauty but also for the wonderfully colorful characters that populate each scene. Very often I was so enthralled with the landscape that I forgot to pay attention to the plot. But then that provides the perfect excuse to return for another show.

The 1990s brought fine cinema from Ireland, as evidenced by *My Left Foot*, *The Field*, and *The Crying Game*. Although some of the actors in these films are not from Ireland, Irish stories set in Ireland resonate with human emotion.

I've always been a huge fan of anything Irish when it comes to cinema, even though early Irish American movies relied on stereotypes and portrayed the Irish as gangsters, law enforcers, and priests. In time the genre changed, introducing the Irish as unconscionable rogues, mischievous fairies, and long-suffering characters, such as you'll find in *The Quiet Man*, *The Molly Maguire's*, *Angela's Ashes*, *The Magical Legend of the Leprechauns*, and *Finian's Rainbow*.

You can probably name at least a half dozen or so Irish-themed movies that you've enjoyed throughout the years. Bing Crosby, first generation Irish American, played a wonderfully sentimental priest in the movie *Going My Way*, while Barry Fitzgerald, Irish-born, splendidly portrayed the pastor. Maureen O'Sullivan, also Irish-born, starred with John Wayne, Irish American, in a love story/action flick produced and directed in Ireland. Filmed in beautiful Connemara, *The Quiet Man* caused millions of people to fall in love with the west of Ireland.

Chicago offers a wealth of venues for any filmgoer yearning for Ireland's emerald-colored pastures, quilted with ancient hedgerows. The camera captures views of old cottages rooted in the charming countryside, unchanged by generations, alongside modern, bustling cities. See for yourself the beauty and diversity of Ireland through the exceptional film opportunities listed.

Irish Cinema: Show Me The Movies!

Chicago Irish Film Festival

Beverly Arts Center
2407 West 111th Street
773/445-3838
www.chicagoirishfilmfestival.com

The Beverly Arts Center sponsors an Irish film festival that runs only six days in March, just before St. Patrick's Day. Be sure to mark your calendars; you'll not want to miss these excellent film produc-

Beverly Irish Film Festival.
(Courtesy of the Beverly Arts Center.)

tions from Ireland. These are not the kind of movies you'll find playing at your neighborhood cineplex but rather are those that give voice to creative Irish independent filmmakers. Phone ahead if you're interested in attending the opening-night reception. You'll meet filmmakers, actors, directors, and critics. If you ever wondered how to make a five-minute film out of hours of footage, participate in one of their workshops. Observe the editing and decision-making processes. Learn how those decisions affect the final cut to create an award-winning short. The Chicago Irish Film Festival has earned its reputation as a showcase for the best in new Irish films.

The Beverly Arts Center has recently introduced a weekly BACinema—a unique mix of the best international, independent, and classic films; keep an eye out for excellent Irish productions. They even provide the popcorn. Films are presented at 7:30 every Wednesday. Call for the film schedule.

The Irish in Film
www.irishfilm.net

This is where you can find Irish movies if you don't have a particular one in mind. *They do not rent or sell movies.* This database provides titles and dates of production, identifies the major players, and offers a short synopsis for each of the films listed—an entire index at your fingertips. Search for movies categorized under biography, history, documentary, Irish Americans, IRA, Irish immigrants, Irish mob, Irish folklore, the Old Country, boxing, and bibliography.

Check out their Web site, list the movies you wish to view, and either rent them at your favorite video store or order direct from pay-per-view. Round up friends and family, wrap your arms around a bucket of microwave popcorn, grab a jug of soda and a pint of your favorite brew, and settle in to enjoy an afternoon or evening of good Irish cinema from the comfort of your living room.

First Friday Film Series

The Irish American Heritage Center
4626 North Knox Avenue
773/282-7035
www.irishamhc.com

The Center offers an all-new First Friday Film Series shown on the evening of the first Friday of each month in their auditorium. This film series is intended to promote Irish and Irish American artistically and culturally significant films that have not received substantial distribution channels in the U.S. market. It also honors the breakthrough work of the great Irish and Irish American film artists, including actors and directors, and promotes an understanding of the influence of this body of work on the perception of Irish culture in American society.

Music Box Theatre

3733 North Southport Avenue
773/871-6604
www.musicboxtheatre.com

For those who prefer film on the big screen, Chicago's Music Box Theatre on Southport offers an amazing array of classic movies and foreign films, including Irish cinema. Some Irish movies from Ireland don't always show up at the neighborhood cinema, so you'll want to be aware on what's being offered at the

Music Box. This lovely old theater, built in 1929, offers a unique viewing opportunity. The architectural style is considered atmospheric, with a dark blue, cove-lit ceiling. Twinkling stars and moving cloud formations suggest a night sky, giving the impression of open-air viewing. All that's missing is a gentle ocean breeze.

Did I mention they use real butter on their popcorn? Definitely worth the price of admission!

Irish Theater: Curtain Up! Dim The Lights!

There's something wonderfully entertaining about the pain and suffering witnessed on the Irish stage. Persistent stereotypes in contemporary Irish American culture continue to entertain the audience with lighthearted references to the drink, the temper, and the sainted mother. It makes us think, makes us laugh, and provides an escape from the real world, all in good fun.

The Irish are a nation of talkers and storytellers. Legends, poetry, stories, and comedy, sprinkled with the grim, tragic realities of political struggles, define the Irish experience. These unique characteristics blend folklore and tradition to create dramatic settings flavored with Irish music, distinctive dialects, and honest banter.

Chicago has traditions rich in Irish culture, and theater has been a vital part of these traditions. Irish theater continues to grow in popularity, nurturing the Irish identity, as evidenced by the variety of theater available in the Chicago area.

Interested in auditioning for a part in a play or working behind the scenes? Give the directors a call; they are always looking for new talent, fresh faces, authentic Irish accents, and creative individuals. Who knows? Some talent agent looking for a new face might just discover you.

Gaelic Park Players

Gaelic Park
6119 West 147th Street, Oak Forest
708/687-9323
www.chicagogaelicpark.org

Gaelic Park, located in southwest Cook County, is home to the Gaelic Park Players, who entertain their audiences with top-rate theater performances. Their mission is to present the best in Irish culture and tradition to the community surrounding Gaelic Park, and to Chicago at large, in the form of Irish drama and comedy. Having recently celebrated their 15th year in the community, their dream of performing in Ireland became a reality in March 2007 with their production of *Buried Again* at the St. John's Theatre in Listowel, County Kerry, Ireland.

The Gaelic Park Players have hosted the annual Acting Irish International Theatre Festival, and they continue to participate in annual Irish theater competitions held throughout the United States and Canada.

Book your tickets for an afternoon or evening performance. Plan to arrive a couple of hours early to relax in their Curragh Pub. Along with your beverage, enjoy delicious pub grub, and, as a bonus, sports telecasts direct from Ireland.

The cozy little theater is located on the second floor of the facility; reach it via the elevator next to the pub. The theater offers a full-service bar where a variety of Irish beer and Tayto brand chips direct from Ireland can be purchased during intermission. When the play is over, take the opportunity to meet the performers; most of them claim Ireland as their birthplace.

Gaelic Park Players stage performances three weekends before Thanksgiving and three weekends after Easter. Check out their Web site or give them a call. Better yet, visit Gaelic Park and see what you've been missing.

Gaelic Park Players.

Become a member of Gaelic Park and keep current on Irish events in and around Chicago. Being Irish is not a requirement for membership. If you've raised a pint or two in celebration of St. Paddy's Day, you're Irish enough.

Seanachai Theatre Company

2206 North Tripp Avenue
773/878-3727
www.seanachai.org

A major player in Chicago's ensemble-driven theater scene, Seanachai (pronounced SHAWN-a-kee; Irish for storyteller) provides compelling productions and programs that focus the energy of artists on the common goal of exceptional storytelling. *The people's stories were at the very core of ancient Irish culture. It was the duty of the seanchai (Old Irish spelling) to keep these stories alive*

In 12 years with 14 productions, they've won five Jeff Awards, eight Jeff nominations, and four Playwriting Awards and nominations—they're one remarkable theater company.

They also host a summer camp for young people to explore the excitement of theatrical storytelling with workshops in acting, voice, and movement. Students learn techniques such as designing props, building sets, and creating costumes. Performances scheduled at the Irish American Heritage Center. Call for details.

Shapeshifters Theatre Company

Irish American Heritage Center
4626 North Knox Avenue
773/282-7035
www.irishamhc.com

They've hosted Irish theater since 1987. As the building renovation crews restored the old school facility, the thespians recruited fellow theater lovers and began

Irish American Heritage Center's Small Theater, Chicago.

bringing Irish history, folklore, and much-loved writings to the stage.

Their large 675-seat auditorium hosts concerts and events on the first floor. A 90-seat theater on the third floor of the center offers raised seating typical of black box theaters. Plan to visit the Fifth Province Pub afterwards to relax and enjoy the open-hearth fireplace and a two-pour Guinness.

Theatre in the Park

Chicago Park District, Sheil Park
3505 North Southport Avenue
312/742-7529, 312/742-7826
www.chicagoparkdistrict.com.

Look out for the Sheil Park Theatre Group's stagings of Irish plays, usually scheduled around St. Patrick's Day. In the past they've performed at the Abbey Theatre in Dublin. Visit their Web site to view their production events.

Music, Dance, and Performance

The Music of Ireland.

The rhythms of Irish music can reach into the soul and lift the spirit, arousing an emotional force that is both powerful and undeniable. Whether you're listening to a melodic dance tune or to a heart-wrenching emigration ballad, its effects often linger well after the notes themselves disappear. It doesn't matter who sings the songs, because the words define the Irish personality—with wit, humor, and passion for the homeland.

We're all familiar with the mournful refrain of "Danny Boy." It's played on every radio station in Chicago on St. Paddy's Day and is the most requested tune in the pub. You'll not find a dry eye in the place, and even those who aren't Irish might long for the rocky cliffs of Kerry where they can frolic among the shamrocks.

The truth is, it's *not* your traditional Irish song. An English lawyer who had never set foot in Ireland wrote it in the early 1900s. Go figure! The song, enjoyed by hundreds of thousands of people on March 17, turns out to be written by an Englishman and popularized in vaudeville by Irish Americans.

How about "My Wild Irish Rose," you say. Surely this must be from Ireland; it covers all the bases—sadness, yearning, and heart tugging. Alas! Published in America in 1899 by Chauncey Olcott, it was written for a New York stage production.

Many of the other songs we grew up with here in America are not from Ireland at all but were written, produced, and distributed in America. While these tunes provide easy listening, they fail to represent the true traditional Irish music.

So what's the real deal? It's the sound and rhythms of the unique instruments along with the lyrical melodies. These instruments are the uilleann pipes (pronounced ILL-en), flute, tin whistle, fiddle, bodhrán (pronounced BOW-rawn), accordion, and mandolin. While the fiddle is the mainstay of Irish music, the mandolin is used for accompaniment. The tin whistle, with its tinlike, high-pitched sound, is probably the least expensive of the Irish instruments but ironically is one of the most difficult to master. The quieter bellows-powered uilleann pipes are preferred in Ireland over the Scottish bagpipes. The bodhrán, a traditional drum made with a wooden frame and goatskin, is the heartbeat of Irish music.

For many folks the only contact they will ever have with Ireland is through the music. If you've always wanted to play an instrument, enroll in one of Chicago's fine Irish music schools. If your singing stirs in others a yearning for a bit of the green, inquire about vocal lessons. Contact the music schools listed. Visit their practice sessions, familiarize yourself with the instruments, and enjoy that personal connection to the Irish heritage.

Irish Music Schools: Rosin Up the Bow!

Comhaltas Ceoltóirí Éireann

www.comhaltas.ie,
www.murphyroche.com

This is a worldwide organization, based in Dublin, Ireland, committed to the preservation and practice of traditional Irish arts such as music, signing, dance, and language. Their annual convention, held in a different city in North America each year, typically features non-stop Irish music sessions right alongside céilí dances that include up to several hundred people. Master musicians present workshops for students while dance masters concentrate on teaching the dance. You don't have to be Irish to participate, for everyone is welcome. If you're interested in joining, visit their Web site for membership details.

Music Schools

Interested in booking performers for an event or taking a class? Contact the schools below for information:

Academy of Irish Music

Irish American Heritage Center
4626 North Knox Avenue
773/725-0300
www.irishamhc.com,
www.academyofirishmusic.org

Noel Rice, founder and dean of the academy, is an Irish flute player. He, along with his gifted music teachers, is credited with teaching traditional Irish music to hundreds of young Chicago students on the fiddle, cello, flute, bodhrán, and tin whistle. Classes are taught at the **Heritage Center. Students range from kindergartners to teenagers.** Emphasis is on group playing, grounded in the Suzuki method. Education includes: weekly practice, a program of workshops, summer school, annual competition, and performances. It is the mission of the academy to create a community of young musicians dedicated to playing and sharing Irish music. Visit their Web site for details.

Anam mór

630/410-8177, 773/562-3150
www.anam-mor.com

Offers young musicians the opportunity to learn an Irish playing style. Beginning with tin whistle or bodhrán, students learn the necessary music skills to play any instrument. Classes in all other instruments require one to two years basic knowledge of the instrument for enrollment. All classes arranged on an individual basis.

Beverly Arts Center

2407 West 111th Street
773/445-3838
www.beverlyartscenter.org

Although it's not an Irish music school, they teach violin, cello, piano, guitar, bagpipe, and harp. Call for details.

Chicago Irish Harp School

Irish Musicians Association performing at Gaelic Park.

773/391-2259
irishharpchicago@yahoo.com

Artistic director Marta Cook has worked to promote the playing of traditional Irish music on the harp throughout the greater Chicago area and beyond and teaches students of all ages and ethnic backgrounds. Students from the school have been featured both as soloists and as members of ensembles at major Irish music festivals throughout the country. They've shone in both national and international competition, with multiple prizes at a world-class level, more by far than any other school outside Ireland.

Marta teaches at the Irish American Heritage Center on Knox Avenue and is available for private lessons. If you don't have access to an Irish harp, she'll make arrangements for a loan.

Irish Musicians Association

Sean Cleland (chairman)
773/412-6166
sean@seancleland.com

Fifty years after its founding, the Irish Musicians Association is still alive with some of Irish music's greatest fiddlers, flute players, and accordion players. The Irish Musicians Association not only teaches children and adults but also promotes the sharing of tunes and styles through music sessions held each week throughout the Chicago area. Visit their Web site for session locations and times.

Irish Music School of Chicago

Sean Cleland, 773/412-6166
www.irishmusicschool.com

Sean Cleland founded the Irish Music School of Chicago in 2003 to pass on the vital, exciting tradition of Irish music to a new generation of students. His pupils learn almost entirely by ear. He teaches not only the tunes and the stories behind the tunes, but also the value of being part of a musician community. Students learn tunes without written music and, often can string together several short tunes in set after set, perform in front of audiences, and help others learn to play. Sean's students have won many top honors in both group and individual competitions across many age categories at the Midwest Fleadh Cheoil (pronounced FLAH-keeol). The school provides lessons on many different instruments for students of all skill levels. Lessons occur at various locations throughout the greater Chicagoland region, including the Irish American Heritage Center, Gaelic Park, the Musical Offerings in Evanston, and St. John Fisher School in Beverly.

IAHC: Classes in harp, fiddle, banjo, guitar, cello, mandolin, mando-cello, bouzouki, Irish flute, and tin whistle. Call 773/282-7035 for schedule.

IAHC and GP: Classes in beginning tin whistle; beginning, intermediate, and advanced Irish fiddle; intermediate bodhrán drum; and voice. Call 708/687-9323 for schedule.

The Musical Offering: Classes in fiddle, banjo, guitar, accordion, concertina, Irish flute, and tin whistle. Learn how to play traditional Irish tunes as part of the Adult Irish Ensemble. Call 847/866-6260 for schedule.

St. John Fisher School: Classes in beginning and elementary tin whistle; and beginning, elementary, and intermediate fiddle. Call the Irish Music School at 773/412-6166 for schedule.

Music sessions
Open to the public and family-friendly. All instruments and all ages are welcome. Join them at the following locations:

The Grafton Pub: 4530 North Lincoln Avenue (Sunday evenings)

Cullen's: 2741 North Southport Avenue (Tuesday evenings)

Grealy's: 5001 West Lawrence Avenue (Wednesday evenings)

Gaelic Park: 6119 West 147th Street (Thursday evenings)

Murphy Roche Music School/Club

11309 West 72nd Street, Burr Ridge
630/662-8611
www.murphyroche.com

Learn to play Irish instruments, master traditional Irish language songs, and perfect the art of stage presence. Curriculum includes teaching poise and performance to both children and adults. A summer camp for kids offers the opportunity to meet professional musicians. Visit their Web site for music instruction CDs and music books.

Murphy Roche School Musicians.

School (*schoil*): Open to adults and children of all ages. Offers instruction in the following: fiddle, banjo, mandolin, button accordion, piano, bodhrán, flute, tin whistle, and voice.

Club: An organization for musicians who play or want to play Irish traditional music; you don't need to be Irish to join. Members meet monthly for music sessions. Newcomers, regulars, families, and friends are always warmly welcomed.

Bands and performance groups: Performs at festivals, concerts, and competitions throughout Illinois and have competed in Ireland at the world-title level. Performance groups of 2 to 16 people are available for céilí, parties, festivals, weddings, picnics, or any get-together. Musicians include players of traditional Irish instruments, singers, and dancers. They also offer dance performance for hire.

Music House, Inc.

2925 West Devon Avenue
773/262-2051
www.musichouseinc.com

Training violinists for over 56 years in Chicago, Music House offers instruction in voice, fiddle, flute, piano, guitar, and other instruments. University-trained violinists versed in the Suzuki method teach the fiddle, utilizing a hands-on approach along with ear training. Perform and compete as a member of their Fiddle Team. Instruction includes bluegrass, Old-Time, Irish, Mexican, Scandinavian, Cajon—all styles of fiddling! Students have performed in music sessions at Chicago's Abbey Pub and have been involved in competitions throughout the state. Proprietor Richard Trumbo is a bandleader who has performed with the Irish music group Mulligan Stew. The school offers private and group lessons. Musical instruments are available to rent.

Old Town School of Folk Music

4544 North Lincoln Avenue
909 West Armitage Avenue
773/728-6000 (both locations)
www.oldtownschool.org

The Old Town School, perhaps the world's largest center devoted to folk music, offers instruction in traditional Irish instruments, as well as vocal training and Irish dance classes. Group and private lessons are available at their two main locations in Chicago. Most instruments are available for rent or purchase at their Different Strummer music store (Lincoln location) or their Little Strummer store (Armitage location)—music stores with a mission. They also do repairs, sell books and CDs, and provide sage musical advice.

Instruments: Classes in Fiddle 4 Irish and Fiddle 4 Irish Forever, mandolin 1 and 2, accordion/concertina, bodhrán drum 1 and 2, and tin whistle. Students can participate in the flute ensemble and Irish ensemble.

Vocal Progamming: Join the women's choir and learn Gaelic songs. Perform with the group at weddings and other festive affairs.

Dance: Courses offered in Irish céilí and set dances, and Irish step dance.

Resources/Music Collection: Located in the basement of the school's Lincoln Avenue location is the Resource Center, where there are thousands of old recordings, books, and magazines. In keeping with the school's overall mission to preserve and present folk and roots music, the collection is open to the public.

Rampant Lion

47 South Villa Avenue, Villa Park
630/834-8108
www.rampantlion.com

Offers bagpipe and drum lessons. They're also the leading retailer of Celtic music in the United States, offering thousands of Irish/Celtic CDs, DVDs, and music books. You'll find fair prices, excellent service, and knowledgeable staff. They sell the practice chanter for lessons and have access to Highland Bag supplies. Call Gayle Baker or visit their Web site for additional information.

World Folk Music Company

1808 West 103rd Street
773/779-7059
www.worldfolkmusiccompany.com

John Devens invites those who share a passion for music to come in, sign up, and enjoy. He encourages all music students to learn to play for the sheer pleasure of it, no matter their age or experience. Instructors offer expertise in fiddle, mandolin, bouzouki, hammered dulcimer, piano, bodhrán, uilleann pipes, and tin whistle.

Second-floor music rooms are set up to resemble recording studios. Children from six months old and up enjoy listening to and participating in a variety of music activities. The store sells, rents, and

repairs instruments. You can purchase Irish music CDs and Irish music books. Their concert/recital venue offers wonderful entertainment. Visit their Web site for dates and times of events.

Music Composition

Accessible Contemporary Music

Seth Boustead (artistic director),
312/493-8726
seth@acmusic.org,
www.acmusic.org

Their goal is to promote classical music by bringing the music of contemporary composers to as wide an audience as possible.

Composer Alive Program: This organization promotes collaboration between composers from different geographical regions by way of their innovative web-based program. Their project includes the work of composer Jane O'Leary, who lives in Galway. Each installment of her piece was recorded at the Chicago Cultural Center and then posted to their Web site. Hearing the pieces in installments and reading the composer comments along the way helps listeners understand the intricacies of music composition. Representatives from this program travel to Galway to perform American music as well as to lead workshops and master classes in conjunction with Jane O'Leary's visit to Chicago.

High School Composers Workshop: This workshop gives talented high school composers the opportunity to work with a professional composer, to hear their piece performed by professional musicians, and then to attend a master class with an internationally recognized composer. Classes meet at the Chicago College of the Performing Arts of Roosevelt University. Call for details.

Silent Films: Accepting submissions for its annual Sound of Silent Film concert at the Chopin Theatre in Chicago. Check ACM Web site for details. Don't miss their scheduled concerts and fundraisers, which often feature Irish music and Irish musicians.

Music Scholarships

Chicago Irish Harp School

Marta Cook
773/391-2259
irishharpchicago@yahoo.com

The Irish Music Foundation sponsors the South Side Harp Scholarship program. Contact Marta for additional information.

Old Town School of Folk Music

4544 North Lincoln Avenue
773/728-6000
www.oldtownschool.org

They offer generous scholarships to those who can't afford to pay registration fees for classes and workshops. Call for information.

Paddy Clancy Music Scholarship

John Gleeson
University of Wisconsin–Milwaukee
Department of Celtic Studies
P.O. Box 413
Milwaukee, Wisconsin 53201

Available to undergraduate and graduate students who wish to pursue studies related to folk songs, sean nós, and traditional singing. Scholarship stipends are $1,500.

Irish Instrument Makers

The Bodhrán Drum

The bodhrán resembles a large tambourine without the jingling parts and has a rather deep and somber sound. An ancient Irish goatskin drum, it is a folk instrument that was originally beaten with one hand, but eventually a cipin, or a small beater, was used to play the bodhrán.

Mike Quinlan Bodhráns

773/481-6962
www.qdrums.com

Mike has been producing bodhrán drums in his workshop for a number of years. When he began playing the drum, he wasn't satisfied with the tourist grade that was given to him by his family, so he looked to upgrade. That led him to research the construction of the drum,

Mike Quinlan's Custom Bodhrán, Chicago.

and he worked to craft a quality product. Endorsed by many fine Irish musicians throughout the country, his bodhráns are gaining popularity. Using birch and maple plywood, each shell is hand-crafted. Shells are typically 14 or 15 inches in diameter, but he can customize the instrument to the player's preference. He places the tuning ring within the drum shell, providing a clean interior. Visit his Web site for ordering information. Orders can take between two and eight weeks to complete.

The Tin Whistle (Pennywhistle)

Although modest in appearance and most economical, the whistle is capable of a range of expression that is truly amazing. It's a simple metallic tube with six holes and a mouthpiece and is similar to the recorder. Its sound ranges between two octaves.

If you've considered leaning the tin whistle, purchase a quality instrument so you won't be discouraged by the performance of the cheaper varieties.

Michael Burke Pennywhistle Company

389 Wells Street, Murphysboro
618/684-5377
www.burkewhistles.com

Dedicated to making the perfect instrument, Mike Burke began developing pennywhistles in 1996. You'll find his handcrafted instruments in the capable hands of many great artists, from solo performers to backup musicians to professional studio musicians who play religious and classical music. Working out of his home with the help of his wife and family, Mike creates a total of 60 different models in various keys and enjoys the distinction of using more kinds of material than any other whistle maker in the world. For those who are considering taking up the pennywhistle, he recommends his Session Ds in brass and aluminum. Uniquely designed, his whistles are available in 20 different keys. Mike's whistles have been featured in such films as *Road to Perdition*, *Gangs of New York*, *The Alamo*, *Ladder 49*, and the *The Passion of the Christ*.

The Irish Fiddle

"Fiddle" is a colloquial term for violin, the first of which were made in Italy in 1549. The fiddle entered the Irish musical scene in the eighteenth century. It has remained a mainstay of Irish traditional music ever since and is considered by most to be the best instrument on which to play traditional Irish music.

Seman Violins

4504 Oakton Street, Skokie
847/674-0690
www.semanviolins.com

The owner, Peter Seman, employs a staff of six experienced professionals, each with extensive training and expert technical skills. Each shop employee is a trained musician and experienced builder of string instruments. In addition, they are all graduates of the Chicago School of Violin Making and have decades of collective experience building, restoring, and repairing string instruments. Many famous musicians have purchased Seman violins and applaud their fine workmanship.

Peter Seman, Seman Violins.

Peter gave me a tour of his shop, where I watched skilled musicians repair, assemble from scratch, and refinish beautiful violins. If you're thinking of purchasing a custom-made fiddle, call Peter or visit the Web site for additional information. Fiddles, violas, and cellos are available to rent. Seman's hosts a variety of violin workshops you'll not want to miss. Visit their Web site for updates and scheduling.

Chicago School of Violin Making

3636 Oakton Street, Skokie
847/673-9545
www.csvm.org

Focuses its instruction on developing basic skills necessary for graduates to enter the field of violin making and repair. Professional graduates are well prepared to join the select number of individuals qualified to make and repair fine stringed instruments.

The Irish Harp (Celtic Harp)

Storytellers, to augment their tales, originally used the harp, the national symbol of Ireland. The Irish believed that music played three major roles in society: it was used to express emotions of laughter or sadness, or for accompaniment into battle. Known as "bards," harpers were honored above all other musicians. Because they maintained the oral tradition of the ancient Celts through their music, the bards held a position of trust and honor. They were quite powerful. This aroused the suspicions of the English crown who considered them to be rebels. During the sixteenth century, Queen Elizabeth I issued a proclamation to hang Irish harpers and to destroy their instruments in an attempt to gain control of Ireland. Harps were burnt and players executed, and, by the late eighteenth century, Irish harpers were nearly extinct. It is only in the last few decades that the harp has gained immense popularity because of Irish musicians like Derek Bell of the Chieftain's. Harp making today is an apprentice program, as it was in the Middle Ages. Harp builders start out as wood-crafters. They work alongside a harp maker for many years. For craft harps (plain folk harps) there are books and prints available to the public.

Lyon & Healy

168 North Ogden Avenue
312/786-1881
www.lyonhealy.com

They manufacture a variety of Celtic (lever harps) in various woods and styles. Many of their salespeople are musicians and are proficient at the harp. Preowned harps are available for sale, and their trade-in program works well for those beginning students who wish to upgrade their purchases within a five-year period (new harps only). You'll want to visit their showroom to see the variety and beauty of these lovely instruments. They also

Lyon & Healy Irish Harps, Chicago.

have on premises a newly constructed concert studio, which provides the final link between harp makers, performing artists, composers, and rapt listeners. The concert hall and adjoining reception area are available to not-for-profit organizations for special events. It's an ideal setting for concerts, lectures, readings, recitals, community meetings, children's performances, and chamber music. Visit their Web site for information.

Irish Dance: Get Your Jig On!

If you've attended Irish festivals, St. Paddy's Day parades, and the after-parade pub celebrations, you've no doubt witnessed the variety and masterful skill that are set forth in Irish dance. From the marvelous display of beautifully crafted costumes to the curly-haired lasses and lads clicking their shoes in aggressive movements to the social dance and the céilí, Irish dance has evolved from an ethnic tradition to an art form with an international stage.

Step dancing is the competitive solo form of Irish dancing now popular because of Riverdance and Lord of the Dance. Each dance contains the same basic elements, and new dances are choreographed all the time; however, actual steps are often unique to each school or dance teacher.

An organized step dancing competition is referred to as a feis ("festival"). Participants in a feis must be students of an accredited step dance teacher. Dance competitions are divided by age and level of expertise. The girls wear distinct but simple costumes for beginners and move into more expensive creations for advanced dancers. Most of the dresses display hand-embroidered Celtic designs. Boys typically wear black pants along with white, black, or bright-colored shirts and possibly a vest. Young men easily get into the competitive dance, for it offers lots of clicks (striking the heels of the shoes against each other) and fast trebles (the toe of the shoe tapping the floor). Irish dance is masculine and loud and quite macho for young men who are looking for the perfect opportunity to impress the ladies, along with mastering footwork, which, by the way, also comes in handy when playing football or delving into amateur boxing. Michael Flatley, "Lord of the Dance," earned the title of world's fastest dancer with 34 taps per second, and as a trained boxer he won the Golden Gloves championship in 1975—fancy footwork put to the test.

The Irish give many reasons for why they hold their arms so still and close to their bodies while step dancing. The one that makes the most sense to me explains that the dancer had little room in which to dance; in Ireland an old door was the perfect stage on which to clog away. Unfortunately, such a small area provided very little room to move around, and the dancers ensured their safety by controlling their movements and not waving their arms.

Set dancing is a form of social dancing, which has been popular in Ireland for over 150 years. Four couples dance sets in a square. Another form of Irish social dance is céilí dancing. This is a different repertoire of dances that includes couples, threesomes, in-lines, squares, and circles, several of these dances in four-couple sets. Céilí dances are often included in competitions, being more precise versions of those danced in pubs and at social gatherings.

If you'd like to learn Irish dance or to participate in social dancing, there are numerous opportunities in the Chicago area. It's especially good for young people because it fosters teamwork, self-discipline, healthy competition, and physical fitness. Irish dancing is great fun, so join in and help to preserve the Irish heritage for generations to come.

Interested in booking performers? Call or visit the Web sites below for details.

Performance School

Spriorad Damhsa

773/478-4171
www.spiritofirishdance.com

This Chicago dance group does not participate in formal competition but instead focuses on creating powerful, artistic performances. While they perform the traditional Irish dances, their repertoire also includes productions choreographed to modern music. Beginners and experienced dancers are welcome. Visit their Web site for booking information.

Irish Dance Schools— Chicago and Suburbs

Anam Mór Academy

630/410-8177
www.anam-mor.com

In Barrington, Libertyville, and Chicago. They also sell secondhand dance shoes, wigs, dresses, shirts, etc.

Blackbird Academy

17054A Oak Park Avenue
Tinley Park, 708/802-0793
www.blackbirdacademy.com

Also has locations in Darien and Oak Lawn.

Cross Keys

708/424-7459
www.crosskeys.org

In Chicago, Lemont, Worth, and Oak Forest.

Dennehy

2555 West 111th Street
773/881-3990
www.dennehydancers.com

This is the school where Michael Flatley learned to dance. They also sell second-hand dresses, shoes, wigs, shirts, etc. Parents' club and newsletter. Visit their Web site for class locations.

Foy

5225 W. Berteau
312/720-3069
www.foyirishdancers.com

Also in Batavia. They sell secondhand shoes and have a newsletter.

Dillon Gavin

735 East Balsam Lane, Palatine,
847/202-0064
www.dillon-gavin.com.

Lavin-Cassidy

6401 West 107th Street, Worth
708/448-6593,
www.lavincassidy.com

Also in Chicago and Naperville. They sell secondhand shoes and dresses. There's a parents' club and senior ladies' céilí.

Mayer

51 South Villa Avenue, Villa Park
630/834-8440
www.mayerschool.com

Also in Chicago, Carol Stream, Elmhurst, Roselle, West Dundee, and Northwest Indiana.

McNulty

8640 West Sunset, Niles
847/698-4434
www.mcnultyirishdancers.com

Also in Chicago, Arlington Heights*, Brookfield, Niles, Elmhurst/Villa Park, Naperville, Libertyville, Glen Ellyn,

Rockford, Crystal Lake*, Gurnee, Oak Park, Palatine, Richmond*, Rockford, Schaumburg*, Villa Park*, and Westchester*. Adult beginners and "boys only" classes in many locations. You can book dance performances and educational programs on topics related to Irish dance. *Call the local park district for schedules.

Mulhern

543 North Country Line Road, Hinsdale
630/789-1127
www.mulhernschoolofirishdance.com

Also in Chicago and Westmont.

Mullane

P.O. Box 31681, Chicago
773/775-9807
www.mullanedancers.com

Also in Oak Forest and Tinley Park.

Irish Dance Performers from Murphy Roche Music and Dance School.

Murphy Roche Dance

11309 West 72nd Street, Burr Ridge
630/662-8611
www.murphyroche.com.

Norton-Healy Academy

420A North York Street, Elmhurst
630/833-3170
www.nortonhealy.com

Also in Oak Park and Chicago.

O'Hare

773/868-0957,
www.ohareirishdancers.com

In Chicago.

Old Town School

4544 North Lincoln Avenue, Chicago
773/728-6000
www.oldtownschool.org.

Sheila Tully Academy

1750 Glenview Road, Glenview
847/998-0066
www.Tullyirishdancers.com

Also in Skokie, Deerfield, Lake Forest, Mt. Prospect, Northfield, River Forest, Wilmette, Winnetka, Oak Park, and Evanston.

Sullivan

815/462-4763

In the southwest suburbs.

Honorable Mayor and Mrs. Daley with the Sheila Tully Dancers.

Sullivan

773/763-7391

In Chicago, Winnetka, and Gurnee

Trinity

2936 North Southport Avenue, Chicago

773/774-5961

www.trinity-dancers.com

Also in Barrington, Bridgeport, Lakeview, South Loop, Arlington Heights, Downers Grove, and Elmhurst. Denise Sabala School of Dance in Lake Zurich, Naperville, Northfield, St. Charles, and Western Springs.

Whelan

773/774-9486

In Chicago.

World Academy

630/789-1128

www.worldacademydancers.com

In Lemont, Western Springs, Oak Lawn, the South Loop, and South Bend.

Céilí and Set Dances

Wherever the Irish settled, dance and music followed. Céilí dancing is an informal and energetic style of Irish group dancing, matched with lively traditional Irish music. If you're looking to join with others in the dance, call the numbers listed below for information. You're guaranteed an evening of fun and good entertainment.

Gaelic Park

Oak Forest

www.ChicagoGaelicPark.org

For adult céilí call 708/535-0597, for adult set dancing call 708/598-5313, and for adult beginners and improvers call 708/671-1221.

Céili Dancing at Gaelic Park.

Irish American Heritage Center

Francis O'Neill Céilí Club

773/282-7035, x10

www.irishamhc.com

All levels welcome, partners not required.

Old Town School

www.oldtownschool.org

Irish céilí and set dances.

Feis (Competition)

All dancers compete according to their age and level of experience. The competitors dance on a stage in front of a judge who grades each independently. Medals are awarded and trophies are presented at the championship levels. Once dancers reach the championship levels, they compete in regional competitions, known as Oireachtas, and ultimately at the World Championships, held annually in Ireland.

What you'll see on your first visit to a *feis* might be viewed as pure mayhem; there are hundreds of competitors, each with at least one adult in tow. But, as the day moves along, you can clearly see the results of hard work and persistence. These dancers love their art and their connection to Irish heritage.

If you have a budding Irish dancer in your family, you might wish to visit one of the following competitions just to get an idea of what is involved; costumes, hairpieces, shoes, etc. can be pricy.

Chicago Autumn Feis

Tinley Park
www.chicagoautumnfeis.com

Chicago Feis

Oak Forest
www.chicagogaelicpark.org

Chicago Pat Roche Feis

Arlington Heights
www.patrochefeis.com

Norton-Healy Feis

Lisle
www.nortonhealyfeis.com

Prairie State Feis

St. Charles
www.prairiestatefeis.com

Irish Dance Feis, First Place Trophy.

Performers and Entertainment: Fire In The Kitchen!

The phrase "fire in the kitchen" describes a remarkable performance of musicians at a Hooley or pub session with tunes that move the spirit and rock the place. You needn't be Irish to love Irish music; a good jig or a rollicking reel can inspire your soul and move your feet no matter what your heritage, because beneath the toe tappin' there's the heart tuggin'—the yearning for homeland and the untold stories of the past. As each generation slips away, the music remains a means of telling those stories. If you've grown up singing songs learned around the kitchen table, then you know how the Irish have celebrated their life through stories and song. And if you've only an ounce of Irish blood circulating in your veins, thiso is music that will speak to you in amazing ways in a language that has no need of language.

Purchase a few CDs from local artists and take yourself to their performances or music sessions. See the true Irish instruments and hear for yourself the powerful, passionate rhythms. Listen to the stories told through song—discover that fire in your soul.

I would be remiss not to mention Chicago's former police chief Francis O'Neill, who saved Irish music from fading into oblivion. Born near Bantry Bay, County Cork, in 1848, O'Neil grew up in an Irish-speaking rural society in which music, song, and dance were an integral part of his life. He and his parents and sisters were all great singers. At a young age he began learning the wooden flute, a skill that would help him some years later in America. He settled in Chicago in 1873 and became the chief of police in 1901. With the help of many devoted collaborators, O'Neill collected over 3,400 pieces of traditional Irish dance music from other displaced Irish, nearly single-handedly saving the vastly undocumented and quickly disappearing traditional music of Ireland, most notably with the 1903 publication of O'Neill's Music of Ireland. Containing 1,850 melodies, it was the largest collection of Irish music ever printed. Chief O'Neill died in 1936, but the musical tradition that he revived lives on forever in his hometown of Chicago, in his native Ireland, and in Irish communities all over the world.

My list does not include all of Chicago's talented Irish performers; an entire book could be written on that topic alone. I've provided the names of a few well-known Irish vocalists and musicians, along with the old masters—those who learned the music in Ireland from their parents and grandparents and who continue to play in and around Chicago. Musicians like Kevin Henry, Malachy Towey, and Albert Neary provide the authentic music from a way of life that is no longer—a unique window into traditional music in the days before the motorcar, the television, and the telephone.

Attend the music sessions where traditional Irish music is played (see the Pub chapter for sessions). Many of these musicians also teach, either privately or through a school. Looking to book Irish performers for a special event? Visit their Web sites for contact information.

If you're planning a party or get-together and need to book Highland pipers or the traditional uilleann piper, I've listed them, along with Irish storytellers (seanchai), a magician, and more. This is not an all-inclusive list by any means, but if you're looking for performers, this will get you started. (The uilleann pipes are the national bagpipes of Ireland, not the Highland pipes, as most people believe. The uilleann is made up of bags, bellows, chanter, drones, and regulators. The bag is inflated by means of a small set of bellows strapped around the waist and the right arm. Dry air powers the reed.

They are difficult to play because the piper must master the art of pumping the bellows, keeping a proper pressure on the bag, using the elbow, and playing the chanter simultaneously—an amazing feat. Played indoors and while sitting down, these pipes are most conducive to joining in on traditional Irish music sessions. In the hands of a skillful piper, the instrument is one of the most haunting and beautiful in all the world.)

Female Artists

Liz Carroll

Irish fiddle
www.lizcarroll.com

When listening to Liz Carroll as she masterfully guides her fingers along the strings of her fiddle, one can only be in complete awe of such amazing talent. Creative genius drives her energy and passion. She composes her own compositions, numbering over 200 tunes, which she performs throughout the world. Liz has amazed the Celtic music world by winning the Senior All-Ireland Championship, and she is one of traditional music's most sought after performers. You can find her playing at festivals, concerts, and teaching master classes.

Marta Cook

Irish harp
773/391-2259, irishharpchicago@yahoo.com

Marta Cook placed first in the All-Ireland competition of 2001 and currently performs in some of the finest venues in the city. Artistic Director of the Chicago Irish

Harp School, Marta teaches classical as well as lever harp.

Marta Cook, Director, Chicago Irish Harp Schools.

Aislinn Gagliardi

Irish harp
www.aislinnmusic.com

Aislinn grew up listening to and falling in love with all kinds of music. Beginning with piano lessons at an early age, she took up the hard at the age of 13. Pursuing her musical passion, she went on to earn a Master of Arts degree in Music and Dance Studies from the University of Wisconsin-Milwaukee., honing her skills on the pedal harp. Traveling to Ireland, she spent a semester at the University of Limerick, furthering her studies in Irish culture, along with music and dance, working closely with renowned Irish harpists. She has appeared as a featured guest on numerous radio shows in Ireland as well as in the U.S., performing both Irish and classical music. She teaches harp lessons from her studio on the Northwest side of Chicago. You can catch her at an Irish music session on any given weekend.

Catherine O'Connell

Vocals
www.catherineoconnell.com

Catherine O'Connell is truly magnificent. Her performances are both powerful and moving. Catherine grew up in Chicago and was voted St. Patrick's Day Parade Queen in 1976. She developed her distinctive style and dramatic stage presence by performing in dozens of pubs, saloons, and cabarets. The Chicago Sun-Times dubbed her the "Maureen O'Hara

Catherine O'Connell, Vocalist, accompanied by John Williams.

Clone." You'll not only be captivated by her pure vocal tones but you'll also be astounded by her smooth emotional delivery. Catherine is available to sing for weddings, funerals, and special events.

Male Artists

Sean Cleland

Irish fiddle
www.irishmusicschool.com

Sean Cleland is a noted Irish fiddle player, Irish music teacher, and bandleader from Chicago. He will perform at any of your events and organize any type of Irish music performance for that special occasion. Sean began teaching Irish music in the early 1980s and established the award-winning Irish Music School of Chicago in 2003. In 1988 Sean founded the influential Irish-Rock band, the Drovers. He lead this cutting-edge band for ten years, during which time they recorded four critically acclaimed records, appeared in two motion pictures, *Backdraft* (1991) and *Blink* (1994), and played hundreds of sold-out shows across the U.S. In 2000 renowned Irish musician Jimmy Keane directed Sean to the band known as bohola, where he went on to record three albums. Sean now devotes himself exclusively to the Irish Music School of Chicago. Under his tutelage, the students have earned top honors in both group and individual contests and have qualified each year to compete in the prestigious world championships (the Fleadh Cheoil na hEireann) in Ireland. Hear Sean's music sessions at Gaelic Park and various pubs around the city.

Gavin Coyle

Vocals, guitar, bodhrán, flute
www.gavincoyle.com

Gavin Coyle grew up amidst the fallout from the troubles in Northern Ireland. At age 14 he won the title of All-Ireland Singing Champion and graduated from St. Mary's College in Belfast with a double major in education and art. He came to the United States in 1995 as an accomplished performer and has been performing in sold-out concerts throughout the area. An accomplished singer and songwriter, he has a broad musical range that covers pop, folk music, and traditional music from his homeland. He has recorded a number of CDs, available in Irish stores throughout Chicagoland, as well as through his Web site. Book Gavin to sing/cantor at weddings and other special events.

Kevin Henry

Flute, tin whistle, uilleann pipes, storyteller (seanchai)
www.cdbaby.com/cd/kevinhenry

Kevin Henry was born outside the town of Tubercurry, Ireland, in 1929 and made his way to Chicago to become one of the founding members of the Irish Musician's Association of America in 1956. An expert in the uilleann pipes and black wooden flute, Kevin plays the tunes and tells the stories of old Ireland. Raised in the shadow of the 1916 Easter insurrection and the subsequent civil war, Henry's recitation style shows the patriotic influence from his schoolmasters. His tone is ardent and undeniable, whether he's speaking about the injustice of the courts, the caste system, or the dangers of the drink. Notably a major influence in the revival of Irish music in Chicago, Kevin has mentored and played with many fine Chicago musicians, including Michael Flatley, Sean Cleland, and Liz Carroll, as well as with other young musicians who seek to find their place in the Irish music community. Kevin's daughter Maggie Healy accompanies him on the reels. Maggie plays flute, fiddle, tin whistle, and bodhrán. The breathing of father and daughter duets is so remarkably precise it is difficult to detect that there are two instruments. Kevin has hosted sessions on

Kevin Henry on the Uilleann pipes.

the South Side of Chicago for over two decades; he sits like the master, uilleann pipes poised, while he plays the black flute in the breathy West of Ireland "rushing" style. Much like his hero, Chief O'Neill, Kevin Henry had dutifully earned his own place in the great tradition of Irish music. Attend one of his sessions on Sunday evenings at Lanigan's Pub on 111th Street and Kedzie, or purchase his CD, and hear for yourself what Irish music should be.

David James

Hammered dulcimer, fiddle, tin whistle, bodhrán
www.tiompanalley.com

David James has devoted his life to preserving many time-honored and cherished Irish musical traditions. Along with mastering many instruments, he writes his own music and has released this material on CDs. David is a three-time All-Ireland Champion on the hammered dulcimer and has won many U.S. Midwest Fleadh titles on the dulcimer and fiddle and has also won trio competitions in traditional singing and newly composed song categories.He teaches part time in South Bend and on Wednesdays and Thursdays at World Folk Music on 103rd Street in the historic Beverly neighborhood of Chicago.

Jesse Langen

Guitar, Irish music, music theory, ear training, composition
www.jesselangen.com

Jesse Langen's constant quest to broaden his musical horizons makes him an inspired and inspiring teacher. His eclectic musical interests, abilities, and accomplishments allow him to draw on a range of traditions and methodologies in any teaching assignment. Jesse is currently pursuing a Doctor of Music (DM) degree in guitar at Northwestern University. He has played in master classes and was a featured soloist with the Chicago Symphony Orchestra. Catch him at music sessions at Greeley's Pub on Lawrence and at the Galway Arms on Clark.

Brendan McKinney

Uilleann pipes, highland pipes, Irish flute, tin whistle
www.chiefoneillspub.com

Brendan McKinney owns and operates Chief O'Neill's Pub and Restaurant in Chicago. He is a champion bagpiper who also grooves on the uilleann pipes, the wooden concert Irish flute, and the tin whistle. Brendan won the championship in Ireland on the highland bagpipes. His wife, Siobhan McKinney, plays the wooden concert Irish flute and the tin whistle and has won an all-Ireland championship for her airs on the flute. Drop into Chief O'Neill's to hear their performances.

Albert Neary

Flute

Albert Neary arrived in America from County Mayo in 1964. He picked up the tin whistle when he was seven, watching the elders and learning their tunes. Music was something he learned by listening—it was all about hearing the tunes, as there was no sheet music. After his arrival in Chicago, Albert developed his love for the flute by joining the Irish Musicians Association and playing music for céilí dancing. When I asked him why all the Irish musicians tap their shoe to the tune, Albert informed me that is the way each musician learns the other's beat or tempo. If a new musician joins in the session, as is often the case, the others will watch his shoe to catch the rhythm. Albert confessed to knowing hundreds of old Irish tunes, and he uses no sheet music. You can find Albert and his flute at the Sunday evening music sessions at Lanigan's

Albert Neary with his traditional black flute.

Pub on 111th Street and on Thursday nights at Gaelic Park's Carraig Pub.

Devin Shepherd

Irish fiddle

773/612-8066

fiddledd8@yahoo.com

Devin Shepherd graduated from Roosevelt University with a degree in music composition and now makes his living teaching and performing Irish music. Charmed by the sounds of Irish music as a young boy, Devin abandoned the classical violin to turn his attention to the Irish fiddle. Under the tutelage of talented musicians such as Kathleen Keane and Liz Carroll, Devin went on to win the Midwest Fleadh Cheoil Irish Music Competition for nine consecutive years. Hear this gifted musician each Sunday evening at the Abbey Pub leading an Irish music session.

Malachy Towey

Bodhrán drum

Malachy Towey hails from County Mayo and has been playing the bodhrán for 77 years. Crafting his first drum in 1930 at the age of 10, he tells how the goat was slaughtered and then given to the kids in the townland. They skinned the goat and then buried the skin with lime in order to remove the goat hair. Seven days later, they dug up the skin, attached the smooth, hairless goatskin to a hoop riddle (used to sift grain), and the rest is history. Malachy has achieved the distinction of being one of Chicago's icons in Traditional Irish music. Using his fingers, instead of the tipper, he produces the rich, rushing style of the masters. Frequently running a damp cloth over the goatskin, he tunes his bodhrán, softening the tone; there are no tuning screws to be found in his instrument. Malachy accompanies his childhood friend Kevin Henry at music sessions, and you can hear his

Malachy Towey with his bodhrán.

music on Kevin Henry's CD. Stop in to Lanigan's Pub on 111th Street and catch Malachy's Sunday sessions. His grandson Stephan Szyman can be seen picking up the beat on his bodhrán, carrying on this fine family tradition.

John Williams

Button accordion, flute, tin whistle, bodhrán, concertina, piano
www.johnwilliamsmusic.com

John Williams delivers brilliant, masterful music on several instruments for any occasion. Internationally regarded as one of the foremost players of Irish music, John is the only American-born competitor ever to win first place in the Senior Concertina category. He started the Celtic supergroup Solas and toured internationally releasing numerous award-winning recordings. He maintains the longest-running weekly music session in Chicagoland on Sunday afternoons at Tommy Nevin's Pub in Evanston. On the silver screen John appears as a bandleader, music consultant, and composer in the Chicago thriller *Road to Perdition*. He's recorded with the London Symphony Orchestra and the Metropolitan Symphony Orchestral and has played at the National Music Hall in Dublin. John balances raising a family, teaching, recording, and performing locally with international concerts featuring his duo with world guitarist Dean Magraw.

John Williams with the button accordion.

Couples and Groups

Baal Tinne

Flute, bodhrán, guitar, keyboards, fiddle
www.baaltinne.com

Baal Tinne is an Irish music group founded by Noel Rice. Their tunes range from traditional rhythm utilizing emotion and tension with just the right amount of charisma. They've managed to artfully orchestrate the traditional with the contemporary without sacrificing the comfortable, familiar sound of Celtic music. Noel plays the flute and tin whistle, his daughter Cathleen Halliburton on fiddle, son Kevin Rice on bodhrán and percussion, Matt Sundstrom on guitar, and Richard Roche on piano and keyboards. Noel also serves as the Director of Academy of Irish Music, and teaches at the Irish American Heritage Center.

Bohola

Accordion, bass bouzouki, guitar, vocals
www.bohola.com

Bohola combines Irish traditional music and its American adaptation. With a name taken from the title of an old tune, *The Bohola Jig*, they play melodies that range from 100-year-old harp pieces, reels, jigs, slides, polkas and barn dances to newly composed pieces in the traditional sense.

Patrick Cannady and Karen Cook Cannady

Uilleann pipes, Irish fiddle
www.myspace.com/piobagusfidil

Patrick Cannady and Karen Cook Cannady were drawn together by their mutual love of Irish traditional tunes and have been performing as a duet since 2002. Their tunes are a mix of knotty, twisted old piping jigs, bouncy fiddle tunes from Sligo, accordion tunes from Clare and East Galway, and many others. Mentored by some of Chicago's great Irish immigrant musicians, Patrick and Karen have attained a solid foundation of technique,

Patrick Cannady with Uilleann pipes and Karen Cook Cannady on fiddle.

style, and repertoire that's essential to playing great, expressive Irish music. Impressed with the early recordings of Edward Mullaney, James Morrison, and John McFadden, they've added new material to their ever-increasing repertoire of dance tunes. They're performed at the Southern California Pipers' Club Tionol, at the Great Northern Irish Piper's Club in the Twin cities, and at Chicago's Celtic Fest. Patrick and Karen are currently booking for events such as céilí dances, parties, concerts, restaurants, and pub performances. They play in music sessions throughout the city. For detailed information about uilleann pipes, visit the Irish piper's club, Na Piobairi Uilleann, at www.PIPERS.IE.

Henhouse Prowlers

Guitar, bass, fiddle, mandolin, dobro, banjo
www.henhouseprowlers.com

Henhouse Prowlers play Bluegrass with a Celtic twist. When we examine the Bluegrass family tree, the Irish influence is interlined tightly within its roots. The street balladry of the people who began migrating to America in the early 1600s is considered to be the root of traditional American music. These folk ballads and intensely personalized tunes are imported from the British Isles as well as Scotland and Ireland. And these guys bring the house down, because they deliver clear Irish tunes that'll take your breath away. They've toured with Mike Leonard, NBC Correspondent, playing accompaniments to his Irish stories. They regularly perform at the Red Line Tap, 7006 North Glenwood Avenue, at the Celtic Knot in

Evanston, at Simon's Tavern, 5210 North Clark Street, and at Pete Miller's in Wheeling. Ben Wright teaches banjo. Contact him at 847/475-0260. Ryan Hinshaw teaches fiddle and classical violin. Contact him at 773/793-6261.

Moore & Broaders

Uilleann pipes, bouzouki, acoustic guitars, vocals

Moore & Broaders style combines instrumentals and vocals in a mixture of traditional and modern music. Jimmy Moore and Pat Broaders are Irish natives who have performed at Kitty O'Shea's in the Chicago Hilton and Towers for the last fourteen years. They're crowd pleasers, particularly when they play their most popular song, *Black Velvet Band*, an old Irish sing-along tune. You can catch these guys six nights a week at Kitty's. Peter Brady, guitar and vocal, fills in from time to time.

Murphy Roche Musicians

www.murphyroche.com

Murphy Roche Musicians perform at festivals, concerts, and competitions throughout Illinois, particularly during the summer months. Their junior bands have competed in Ireland at the world title level.

Musician Referral Service

The Old Town School of Folk Music

Jenna Murfin, 773/751-3326
www.oldtownschool.org

Looking for soloists, bands, dance instructors, callers or workshop leaders? Look no more, because the Old Town School has it all, and, at affordable prices. Musicians are available for weddings, picnics, festivals, corporate events, holiday parties, and children's parties.

Highland Bagpipers

The City of Chicago Pipe Band

Patrick Lynch, 773/875-6812
www.chicagopipeband.com

Founded as a competition and instructional band, the band is committed to offering free bagpipe lessons to anyone aged 8 to 18. The band is also available for any and all performances include parades, weddings, Celtic and music festivals, and more.

Chicago Highlanders

Art Skwerski, 708/383-2994
www.chicagohighlanders.org

With their pipes and drums, the Chicago Highlanders are just the group for your parade or festival.

City of Chicago Pipe Band.

Chicalba Bagpiping

630/534-4964
www.chicalba.com

Chicalba Bagpiping is available for weddings, parties, funerals, and corporate events.

Paul S. Palmer

312/749-3940
www.bagpipes4hire.com

Paul Palmer has more than 25 years experience on the Great Highland Bagpipes. Paul accepts bookings for funerals, weddings, Irish-Scottish music, surprise events, and parties.

Shannon Rovers Irish Pipe Band of Chicago

773/792-3131
www.shannonrovers.com

The Shannon Rovers have been a cultural fixture in the Chicago area for over 75 years. From parades to politics, from weddings to funerals, this group brings the passion of Irish music with them.

Emerald Society of Illinois

www.emeraldsocietyofillinois.org

An organization comprising Irish-American police officers from throughout the State of Illinois, the Emerald Society of Illinois is available for events throughout Chicago.

The Firefighters Highland Guard

630/330-3484
www.napervillepipesanddrums.org

The Firefighters Highland Guard was founded in September 2003 as a way to show respect for those lost in the 9/11 attacks and to honor our fallen firefighters as well as those in the military. They play for festivals, parades, military funeral services, monument dedications, retired firefighter memorials, funerals, and weddings The group comprises eight pipers and eight drummers.

Pipes and Drums of the Chicago Police Department

www.pdcpd.org

Available for all events, the Pipes and Drums of the Chicago Police Department is over 30 members strong, with players from various cultural and ethnic backgrounds. The only prerequisite to join is that you be an active sworn member of the CPD.

The Chicago Stock Yard Kilty Band

www.sykb.com

The Chicago Stock Yard Kilty Band is one of the oldest continuous pipe bands in the United States. They are available for all events.

The Glengael Bag Pipe Band

www.glengael.com

Committed to the rich Celtic heritage of bagpipe music, the Glengael Bag Pipe Band brings entertainment and tradition to Chicago audiences through community events, competitions, and private engagements. They are available for weddings, birthdays, funerals, benefits, parades, grand openings, and private parties.

Midwest Pipe Band

www.mwpba.org

Midwest Pipe Band's Web site is your online resource for information on piping in the Heartland. You'll learn recent news on events, competitions, and rules. You can also locate band members and make contact with them.

Storytelling (Seanchai)

Seanachai Theatre Company

2206 North Tripp Avenue
773/878-3727
www.seanachai.org

A Chicago theatre steeped in the Irish storytelling tradition. They sponsor a summer camp for young people. The camp explores the excitement of theatrical storytelling with workshops in acting, voice and movement combined with techniques such as designing and building props, sets and costumes.

Leanne Johnson

Byron
815/979-9196
www.storytelling.org/Leanne

Leanne combines her love of music with her passion for storytelling to bring new life to old tales, original stories, poetry, and songs for listeners of all ages. Instruments that emerge in performance include Celtic harp, bodhrán drum, and assorted rattles and noisemakers. Visit her Web site for details and booking.

Susan O'Halloran

Evanston
866/997-8726
www.susanohalloran.com

She is the author of several books and produces performances and videos for high school through adult audiences. Susan has mastered the Irish art of telling stories that are funny and heart wrenching at the same time. Visit her Web site for details.

Genesis at the Crossroads

773/929-0224
www.gatc.org

An organization dedicated to showcasing ethnic artists who create and perform vocal, instrumental, dance, literary, and visual works of art. Their programs have included Irish storytelling and traditional music. Visit their Web site for performances scheduled throughout the year.

Illinois Storytelling

Aurora
630/877-0931
www.storytelling.org

Their mission is to connect generations, nurture communities, and celebrate diversity through stories. Visit their Web site for details.

Liz Warren

www.mc.maricopa.edu

Liz teaches an online course in Irish storytelling tradition. The course explores the history and practice of storytelling in Ireland; Irish myths, legends, folktales and humorous tales; great storytellers and story collectors of the past and present; modern masters of Irish storytelling; and how to research, develop and craft Irish stories for telling. Visit her Web site for class syllabus.

Magic, Variety, and Television

Irish Billy

Magic and Variety Show
815/566-6717
www.irishbilly.com

If you're looking for good, wholesome Irish family entertainment for your next party, look no further. Born and raised in County Meath, Ireland, Bill began his career as part of an amateur variety group in Ireland. The group went on to win the National Championship, and Bill won an individual award for his juggling performance. He wrote a children's song titled,

Happy Street, which won an award for a "Songs of Conscience" project funded by the U.S. Department of Education. The contest was held to promote positive lyrics/messages in music for kids. His magic and variety show, featuring an action-packed performance of magic, music, juggling, comedy, air guitars, and puppets, promises to delight and entertain. He offers performances for all events and organizations, including children's parties, adult variety shows, corporations, schools, daycare centers, holiday parties, family reunions, and more. Book early with Billy; his calendar fills quickly.

Irish Billy, Performer/Magician.

Tom & Maggie O'Little

Those Funny Little People Enterprise, Inc.

7501 South Quincy Street, Willowbrook

630/325-3320
www.thosefunnylittlepeople.com

You've seen these two cavorting with many of Chicago's fine politicians each year at the St. Patrick's Day parade. Tom & Maggie O'Little provide just the touch of humor needed for your St. Paddy's Day event. Check their Web site for pictures and information.

Maggie Daley with "Those Funny Little People," St. Patrick's Day Parade, Chicago.

The Jakers! An Animated Irish Children's Story

WTTW-TV, Channel 11, and WYCC-TV, Channel 20
www.pbskids.org/jakers/

Jakers! Raises the bar for state-of-the-art animated children's shows. Each episode of *Jakers!* is set in two distinct places and times. The most significant location, and the heart of the show, is Raloo Farm in the rural Irish village of Tara in the 1950s.

Young Piggely Winks and his friends have all kinds of adventures and learn the important lessons in life. Children and adults alike will delight in the Irish accents and the beautiful animation. The thatched cottages, rolling hills, and nuances of old Ireland will keep you glued to the screen. Visit their Web site for interactive games for children, as well as show times in other cities. *Jakers!* children's books are available for purchase on the Web site and through Amazon.com.

Organizations and Clubs

Sculpture of "Grainne." Gift from Chicago's Sister City, Galway, Ireland.

C hicago is no Second City when it comes to the Irish. From the rocky cliffs of Ireland to the Great Plains of the Midwest, the immigrants found their way to this city on the shores of Lake Michigan. They arrived in Chicago with visions of establishing communities where they could raise families, find work, and become American citizens. The Irish are among the best educated and most liberal people in the world and are well represented in law, medicine, academia, and other prestigious positions. They've established clubs where they play their music, dance, and socialize. Because of their long history of suffering and sacrifice, the Irish have always offered assistance to those in need and, as a result, have created some of the finest organizations in the U.S., many of them based right here in Chicago.

Here's your opportunity not only to help others but also to get connected with the Irish community. Honor your ancestors who dedicated their loyalty and energies to this great city and join the Irish community to celebrate a heritage rich in culture and tradition. You'll not only expand your social circle but you'll also enjoy the company of those who share your love for everything Irish.

Irish Organizations and Clubs

American Conference for Irish Studies

www.acisweb.com

An organization that serves to promote and recognize excellence in Irish studies. Membership is open to those who are affiliated or retired from an academic career and all individuals who are interested in expanding their knowledge and appreciation of Irish Studies. They've established an electronic guide to Irish Studies in the United States, which can be accessed through their Web site.

Ancient Order of Hibernians

Division 32 (North Side)
www.aooh.org
John F. Kennedy Division 59 (South Side)
www.aohchicago.com

The AOH was formed in Ireland in 1565 to protect the Catholic priests, who risked death for practicing their faith in occupied Ireland, and later when the dreaded Penal Laws were implemented. Penal laws eliminated Irish Catholics from the political, social, and economic life of their own country. With their religion outlawed and their clergy on the run, secret societies like the AOH were formed to protect the values at stake. The present-day AOH is for men 16 years and older who are practicing Roman Catholics of Irish birth or Irish descent through either parent and who are citizens of the United States or who have declared their intentions to become citizens of the U.S. The purpose of the organization is to promote Irish values and culture through friendship, unity, and Christian charity. They provide scholarships for elementary and high school students and aid for children with terminal diseases and victims of disaster. Visit their Web sites for membership information.

Celtic Women International

www.celticwomen.org

Organized to honor, celebrate, and promote Celtic women and their heritage. They offer socializing, networking, and opportunities to build relationships through their cultural activities and annual conferences. You don't need to prove direct descent from Irish ancestors in order to join or participate in events. Join their Chicago branch, which meets every third Tuesday at the Irish American Heritage Center, to meet extraordinary Celtic women. Visit their Web site for details

Chicago Irish Brotherhood

708/606-6700
www.chiirishbro.org

Hosts annual events to support the Illinois Fire Safety Alliance's Camp I and Me, the Special Olympics, and the Make-A-Wish Foundation. Established over a decade ago, the Chicago Irish Brotherhood is an extremely efficient and effective organization that relies on members and associates to generate big checks for worthy causes. Visit their Web site for upcoming events and information.

Chicago Irish Immigrant Support

640 North LaSalle Street, Suite 390
312/337-8445, 888/353-2447
www.ci-is.com

If you have any questions regarding Irish or American citizenship, this is the organization you'll need to contact. They provide a caring and supportive forum for young Irish immigrants by offering free and confidential assistance with citizenship, adjustment of status, and other immigration related issues. They also host workshops for those who wish to apply for a DV Lottery, providing green cards to successful candidates. A full-time chaplain from County Clare, Ireland, provides 24-hour pastoral care and support to the community. Join in their annual golf outing held in June; everyone is welcome to participate. Visit their Web site for details.

The CIIS has organized a venue for senior citizens to come together, relax, and take part in social activities. Called the Active Retired Club (ARC), they cater to Irish and Irish-American seniors who wish to meet others who share Irish heritage. The agenda includes guest speakers and a variety of entertainment. Meetings are held at the Irish American Heritage Society and Gaelic Park. Call Breandán 312/337-8445 for details.

Chicago Rose of Tralee

11137 South Artesian Avenue
773/239-3927
www.chicagoroseoftralee.com

Their mission is to provide enrichment opportunities that will encourage young women of Irish descent to be exemplary role models for tomorrow's youth and to make a positive difference in the world. Girls ages 5-12 participate in Rosebuds, young women ages 13-17 as Rose Petals, and the Rose Contestants are ages 18-27. The Rose winner will receive an all expenses paid trip to Ireland and the opportunity to be an ambassador of Chicago's Irish community.

Chicago Sister Cities International Program, Inc.

Chicago Department of Cultural Affairs
78 East Washington Boulevard
312/744-8074
www.chicagosistercities.com

In 1997 Chicago adopted Galway as its sister city. A gift from the City of Galway to the City of Chicago stands in Heritage Green Park, 610 W. Adams St. (across the street from Old St. Pat's Church). The sculpture *Grainne* ("Grace") by Maurice Harron stands as a tribute to the many thousands of Irish who immigrated to America. Familiar with the tragic story of the Great Famine, the artist wished to express something of the other story of Ireland's past. Until the year 1600, Ireland had its own very distinctive Gaelic culture, religion, legal system, economy, and social system. The sculpture of the young girl is meant to symbolize Ireland's very different society before it was destroyed. She is dressed in a voluminous dress and cloak. The formal, elaborate hairstyle is that of a young princess. The base of the sculpture is derived from the famous Turoe Stone, a Celtic pagan monument from County Galway and dates from about the time of Christ.

Look for Sister Cities many year-round activities. See the chapter on events for details and visit their Web site for updates.

Consulate General of Ireland Chicago

400 North Michigan Avenue
312/337-1868
www.irishconsulate.org

While not a club or organization, the consulate provides services in 20 states in the Midwest and the South. Their services include Irish citizenship, passports, and visas to Ireland, as well as consular assistance to Irish citizens with regard to their immigrant status in the U.S. The office on Michigan Avenue is open from 10 am to 12 pm, Monday through Friday.

Emerald Society of Illinois

www.emeraldsocietyofillinois.org

An organization of Irish-American police officers throughout the state. The purpose is the promotion of Irish culture and goodwill through various social events. They sponsor children's Christmas parties and march in the St. Patrick's Day parades downtown and on the Northwest and South Sides.

Gaelic Fire Brigade

8404 South Kedzie Avenue
773/778-5542

Fraternal organization on the city's South Side for firefighters of Irish heritage. Their activities include golf outings, summer barbeques, picnics, and dinner parties.

Gaelic Park

6119 West 147th Street, Oak Forest
708/687-9323
www.chicagogaelicpark.org

South Side's headquarters for Irish sports and culture since 1985. The 50-acre compound offers two ballrooms, a performing arts center, a pub, meeting rooms, and a regulation Gaelic football and hurling field. Delicious meals and music sessions are available in the pub. After that, you can enjoy céilí dancing in their ballroom. You need to check this place out to believe it—you could spend the day and enjoy every second!

Carraig Pub, Gaelic Park.

Good Morning Ireland Foundation of Chicago

773/817-4305
www.gmifofchicago.com

Formed in August 2004 through the Good Morning Ireland Radio Show. They've held fundraisers for breast cancer and for a children's hospital in Dublin. Their events are held at one of the big downtown hotels every year. Visit their Web site to see the date and location of their next big one.

Ireland Network

www.ireland.zant.com

A Chicago-based organization created to develop business networking and social opportunities among Irish-born professionals in the Chicago area. This group holds an annual black-tie ball on the last Saturday in February. Contact Donal O'Brien at DONAL.OBRIEN@BRYANCAVE.COM.

Irish American Alliance

9231 South Roberts Road,
Hickory Hills
708/598-5999
www.chicagoirishamericanalliance.co
mwww.chicagoiaa.org

A social club on the South Side of Chicago established in 1990. The club has over 200 active members and welcomes new members. Members include the Irish—born both in Ireland and in America—and those of non-Irish heritage. Activities include parade participation, trips to baseball games, picnics, golf outings, membership meetings, and a host of other activities. Visit their Web site for details.

Irish American Cultural Institute

773/238-7150
www.iaci-usa.org

Join the IACI and become a part of an organization grounded in the culture and traditions of Ireland. Their programs offer cultural experiences for teenagers; lectures and performance series featuring Irish artists, historians, and storytellers; fellowships in Irish Studies; and so much more. The President of Ireland is one of its patrons. Visit their Web site for details.

Irish American Democrats

www.irishamricandemocrats.org

Raises the public interest in Irish political and economic issues. Join and become a member of this prestigious organization, founded in 1996, and help to expand the Irish American influence in Congress and in state government.

Irish American Heritage Center

4626 North Knox Avenue
773/282-7035
www.irishamhc.com

Fosters the practice, study, and celebration of Irish, Celtic, and Irish American cultural traditions. You'll find two theaters, an authentic Irish pub, a social center, a museum, a library, dance/music studios, and meeting rooms. Visit their Web site for their ongoing activities.

Irish American Heritage Center's Fifth Province Pub.

Irish American Republicans

www.IrishGOP.com

A national organization dedicated to promoting the principles of the Republican Party and to building Republican support among the 45-million-strong Irish American community. They also support justice and peace in Ireland.

Irish American Unity Conference

815/667-4939
www.iauc.org

Many Irish and Irish-Americans live for the day when Ireland will be one united Ireland, free of domination by Britain. Organizations such as the IAUC work to help move this along by supporting American political candidates who bring pressure on England to withdraw its troops from Irish soil. Membership is open to anyone who shares these views. Visit their Web site for details and get involved in the democratic process to unite Ireland.

Irish Fellowship Club of Chicago

815 25th Avenue, Bellwood
www.irishfellowshipchicago.com

Established in 1902, this organization is dedicated to preserving and promoting Irish heritage, culture, and values in Chicago's Irish community. Since 1978 the Foundation has awarded thousands of need-based grants to Catholic high school students of Irish descent. The club comprises the brightest Irish-American minds and the stoutest Irish-American hearts in Chicago. Visit their Web site for membership information.

Irish Freedom Committee

www.irishfreedomcommittee.net

A thriving and growing activist group dedicated to educating the public on a number of issues pertaining to British occupation in Ireland. Read their position on the media's take of Ireland's so called "religious war" and participate in their annual anniversary commemoration of the 1916 Easter Rebellion. If you're interested in learning more about the Irish Freedom Committee and getting involved in their Chicago chapter, visit their Web site. .

Legion of Mary

2315 West Augusta Boulevard
773/235-9327
www.legionofmarytidewater.com/blog/

A lay Catholic association founded in Dublin in 1921 and established in Chicago in 1933 by Mary Duffy. The legion's members participate in the life of the parish through visitations to families and to the sick, both in their homes and in hospitals, and through collaboration in every apostolic and missionary undertaking sponsored by the parish. Every legionary is required to carry out a weekly apostolic work in the spirit of faith and in union with Mary. Membership is open to priests, along with religious and laypeople who wish to associate themselves with the legion by undertaking a service of prayer. Speak to your parish representative for additional information, or call the number listed.

North Side Irish Fire Brigade

6240 West Addison Street
773/545-3883
www.north sidefirebrigade.com

A fraternal organization on the city's North Side for firefighters of Irish heritage.

Northwest Side Irish Organization

773/640-8221
www.northwestsideirish.org

Founded in 2003, the NWSI supports two charitable events a year and an annual St. Patrick's Day parade in March. Visit their Web site for events and membership.

Old St. Patrick's Church

700 West Adams Street
312/648-0121
www.oldstpats.org

Founded by Irish immigrants in 1846, Old St. Pat's is Chicago's oldest public building and a treasured historic landmark. A Special Events Department was formed to create fundraising opportunities that serve to entertain a diverse audience while at the same time generating significant capital to support operational costs. You don't have to be a member of the Church to participate; everyone is welcome. Visit their Web site for details on all events.

Sons and Daughters of Erin

Tara Davlin, Springfield Chapter,
217/787-9045
tara@davlinconsulting.com

A society of men and women dedicated to the preservation of the customs and history of Ireland and her people. They include, but are not limited to, people of Irish descent. The organization aims to include all who also share this interest. If you'd like to create a Chicago chapter, call Tara for details.

South Side Irish Organization

773/393-8687
www.southsideirishparade.org

Supports numerous charitable foundations throughout the year with proceeds from their South Side Irish Parade. Visit their Web site for details.

St. Baldrick's Foundation

888/899-BALD
www.stbaldricks.com

Although events are often held in Irish pubs, you don't have to be Irish to join in this event. The name is a whimsical twist on St. Patrick's Day, and their events (no longer just in March) bring folks together to have their heads shaved to raise funds for childhood cancer research. There are a number of ways to donate: shavees collect donations from friends, family, and associates, or you can donate via their Web site, phone, or check. Organize an event as a barber or shavee, volunteer, sponsor a participant, or make a tribute or memorial gift.

St. Patrick's Missionary Society

1347 West Granville Avenue
773/973-3737
www.spms.org

A society of Catholic priests who work to spread the Gospel throughout the world. If you are interested in attending a retreat in beautiful Glendalough, located in the mountains of County Wicklow, contact Father Michael Rodgers, Brockagh, Gelndalough, County Wicklow, Ireland. Weekday retreats or a one- to three-months' stay in Ireland are offered.

St. Patrick's Residence

1400 Brookdale Road, Naperville
630/416-6565
www.stpatricksresidence.org

Served by the Carmelite Sisters for the aged and infirm. Call for information on nursing care, job, or volunteer opportunities.

The Ireland Funds— The Global Philanthropic Network for Ireland

205 West Wacker Drive, Suite 1400
www.irlfunds.org

Their mission is to be the largest worldwide network made up of both people of Irish ancestry and friends of Ireland that is dedicated to raising funds to support programs of peace and reconciliation, arts and culture, and education and community development throughout the island of Ireland. They support a variety of programs, among them the Special Olympics, 9/11 Disaster Relief Fund, Irish Dogs for the Blind, Samaritans, and Teachnet Ireland. Visit their Web site to view the other programs that they support.

The Irish American Partnership

800/722-3893
www.irishap.org

With over 18,000 members throughout the U.S., this group sponsors a variety of events to fund the purchase of new books for schools in Ireland. They encourage Irish Americans to go back to their roots, to the villages that their ancestors came from, and give something back to the young people who live there today. The honorary chairman, Alderman Edward M.Burke, participates in their Chicago events. Breakfast events and golf outings are among two of their fundraisers. Participate in their extraordinary golfing experience conducted on behalf of education and job creation in north and south Ireland. One-day amateur tournaments are held at the Beverly Country Club in Chicago and are followed later in the year by the Grand Championship Tour to Ireland.

The Irish Children's Fund

55A West St. Charles Road, Villa Park
630/833-1910
www.icfkids.org

Take this opportunity to welcome a child into your home for a summer. The ICF arranges for boys and girls, ages 11 and 12, Protestant and Catholic from Belfast, Ireland, to travel to Chicago, Northwest Indiana, or Indianapolis lodge with a host family for eight weeks in the summer. Friendships are formed, lives are positively influenced, and each of these children benefits from the experience in America. The ICF welcomes inquiries from all families, young couples, single women, empty nesters, and retirees. Visit their Web site for details.

U.S.–Ireland Alliance

2800 Clarendon Boulevard, Suite 502 West, Arlington, Virginia 22201
www.us-irelandalliance.org

Connects the next generation of American leadership with Ireland by fostering a commitment to peace and prosperity among Irish and American leaders. The organization administers scholarships to graduate students who exhibit exemplary academic achievements and a commitment to leadership and community service.

West Suburban Irish

Naperville
630/853-9461
www.wsirish.org

Works to enhance family life through Irish traditions. This not-for-profit organization sponsors the St. Patrick's Day Parade, Irish Mass, and Emerald Dinner and makes donations to charitable organizations such as St. Baldrick's Foundation and Naperville Responds. If you live in the western suburbs of Chicago and are looking to join a worthwhile organization, visit their Web site or give them a call.

Young Irish Fellowship Club turns out in style for the West Suburban Irish Parade.

Young Irish Fellowship Club of Chicago

312/902-1943
www.youngirish.com

A not-for-profit philanthropic and volunteer organization. For over 25 years they have raised money through planned events for Chicagoland charities. They host the largest St. Patrick's Day party in Chicago, scheduled for the Friday before St. Paddy's Day. The club is open to everyone. Check out their Web site for their year-round activities.

County Clubs

Become a member of an organization representing the county in Ireland where your family originated. Join in their monthly meetings, annual conventions, golf outings, race track events, casino nights, dinner dances, Christmas parties, and summer picnics. Reserve a spot on the Irish float at the South Side Parade with the Kerry Club. Some group meetings alternate between the Irish American Heritage Center and

Young Irish Fellowship - Forever Green.

Gaelic Park. Their fundraisers support local charities, provide scholarships, and assist those in need. Family events are scheduled, and children are welcome. Call for membership information and details.

Clare: Martin Falsey, 708/424-0618
Donnegal: Frank Bradley, 815/464-1414
Down: Ann Quinn, 708/599-6230
Galway: Kathleen Cook, 847/885-7795
Kerry: John O'Connell, 708/489-6727
Mayo: Tess Reaney, 708/424-4995
Roscommon: Eileen Healy, 847/966-0499

Business Opportunities

IDA Ireland

77 West Wacker Drive, Suite 4070
312/236-0222
www.idaireland.com

An Irish government agency with the responsibility of securing new investment from overseas in manufacturing and internationally traded service sectors. Over 1,000 overseas companies have established opportunities. Ireland offers the lowest corporation tax rate in Europe at 12.5%. If you've been thinking of moving your business overseas, visit their Web site for additional information.

IAHC

4626 North Knox Avenue
773/282-7035
www.irishamhc.com

Entering the old building brought back fond memories. Forty years ago it was called Mayfair Junior College, where I attended night school, and now it's home to Chicago's Irish. The building was constructed in the 1920s and served as a Chicago Public School for 40 years before becoming one of the City Colleges in the 1960s. The Irish Heritage Society purchased the building in 1987 when a man named Hughie O'Hare decided that Chicago's Irish deserved a place to call their own. So the money was raised to buy the old building on the corner of Wilson and Knox. This antiquated converted school has been filled from basement to rafters with all things Irish.

The Irish American Heritage Center holds the distinction of being *the* gathering place to celebrate Irish culture, music, dance, literature, and theater. Open to the public, the center includes a new library, a beautiful museum, a large auditorium, an authentic Irish pub, and dozens of classrooms where Irish step dancing schools offer lessons. Beginning, intermediate, and advanced classed in Irish pronunciation, conversation, and reading take place a couple of nights a week, as well as on Saturdays. The center also offers classes on Irish history.

Irish American Heritage Center, Chicago.

Inside the center you'll find beautifully crafted Irish design work—check out the classic Celtic knots border circling the lobby area. There's also a shop where you can purchase clothing and books.

The Irish on Knox Avenue intend to keep your toes tappin', your vocals hummin' and your spirits soarin' in sheer delight. Head off to the Center for a genuine Irish experience. Visit their Web site for additional offerings; new events are added weekly. Become a member and

The Irish American Heritage Center's Children's Library.

receive E-mail updates. Don't miss this opportunity to experience Irish heritage and culture at its finest.

Library

Prepare for a surprise when you step into the second-floor library. An impressive Celtic border, designed and hand-painted by artist Edward Cox, wraps around the ceiling; names of well-known Irish and Irish American literature icons, such as Brendan Behan, F. Scott Fitzgerlad, Sean O'Casey, Flannery O'Connor, George Bernard Shaw, Oscar Wilde, William Butler Yeats, C.S. Lewis, Henry James, Joyce Kilmer, Edgar Allan Poe, Bram Stoker, Arthur Conan Doyle, John Steinbeck, and Veronica Guerin, have been crafted in Old Irish script. This border serves as an invaluable way of learning about Irish and Irish American leaders who established academic institutions, founded movements, and spread ideas that have changed Irish American culture forever. Names of the individuals who signed the Irish Proclamation in Dublin in the year 1916 grace the entrance. The library, built entirely by volunteers, showcases metal bookshelves encased in richly grained oak and maple. A Connemara-green-colored marble counter spans the checkout area, and an entire wall of windows provides light for easy viewing in every nook and cranny. You'll not want to miss one corner of this amazing library.

You'll find books dealing with every aspect of Irish and Irish American life. Patrons may access reference books, histories, novels, plays, poetry and the An T-Athair Liam MacGabhann collection of

Irish-language books. Other media include Irish and Irish American periodicals and newspapers, CDs, DVDs, videos, cassettes, and phonographic albums. Original sheet music from the American stage dating from the early 1900s offers the unique opportunity to reminisce.

Ask to see the special collections; these original volumes are not available at any other library. Check out their media center, where any lectures you've missed will have been taped and categorized for your convenience. You'll also be interested to search their genealogy collection, which even includes information on the Scotch-Irish.

Children will delight in the section designed especially for them. Pint-sized tables and chairs invite them to sit and page through the lovely illustrated books. Names of characters from Irish Literature grace the borders that weave around the room. Designed to include the four cycles of literature—mythological, Ulster, Fenian, and historical fairy and folk tales—these hand-scripted details educate visitors about the wealth of literature available for loan. And it's not only Irish books; their collection also includes a variety of ethnic titles so children of different nationalities feel welcome.

Visit their Web site. Participate in their programs. You don't need to be Irish to enjoy good books, and you certainly don't need proof of the green, because everyone is welcome.

Museum

Acquisitions include a magnificent collection of Belleek Parian China; a tapestry by Lily Yeats, sister of W.B. Yeats; a historic chair commissioned by the Irish Fellowship Club of Chicago on the occasion of the visit of U.S. President William Howard Taft on St. Patrick's Day, 1910; a square grand piano dating from the late nineteenth century; an exquisite collection of Irish lace; the first organ from St. Patrick's Church in St. Charles, Illinois; and a series of historic maps showing the Irish contribution to European culture from the sixth to the twelfth centuries.

You'll also find old Irish coins from 1928. The Euro coin is new to Ireland, introduced in 2002. Old Irish coins were unique. Designed by W.B. Yeats, each coin was inscribed with the Irish harp on one side and an agricultural theme featuring animals and birds on the flip side.

A facsimile of the Book of Kells is available for viewing. An ornately illustrated manuscript produced by Celtic monks around ad 800, it is one of the most lavishly illuminated manuscripts to survive from the Middle Ages. It contains the four gospels of the Bible in Latin, along with prefatory and explanatory matter decorated with numerous colorful illustrations and illuminations. The original book was written on stretched calfskin; it's estimated that 185 calves' skins were used. The glowing colors of the illustrations were achieved with an astonishing range of pigments, from crushed oak apples to lapis lazuli to beetles' wings. The original is on permanent display at Trinity College in Dublin. So if you're not planning a trip to Dublin anytime too soon, then this is the next best thing. Call the Irish American Heritage Center to arrange a museum tour.

Genealogy

Genealogy assistance and resources for finding and documenting your family tree are available the last Sunday of every month from 1 to 3 pm. Free to members. Contact Brian Donovan at 773-282-7035. The IAHC is interested in capturing Irish experiences in an Irish History Depository. Call the Center for more information.

Theaters

The first-floor theater contains 680 comfortably cushioned seats, upholstered in deep green. Look close enough at the brass plates on the front row seats and you'll see a familiar name of someone who helped fund the renovation—Richard M. Daley. Plays by the great Irish dramatists, including Sean O'Casey and J.M. Synge, have been performed in this theatre.

Their Shapeshifters Resident Theatre Company is open to actors, support people, and anyone interested in learning about the theater and working on a production. They host two main stage productions per year and two to three one-act plays. Call the IAHC for information on what's in the works. The Shapeshifters Theatre Company has toured a number of summer festivals and has been involved in the Acting Irish International Theatre Festival, an annual event whose location alternates between a U.S. and a Canadian host city every year with its goal of celebrating the traditions of Irish stage.

You'll find a smaller theater on the third floor, where theater groups from throughout Chicago—not only Irish ones—are invited to perform their craft. Check the schedule for upcoming events.

Don't miss their Salon Concerts. These presentations not only offer the ambiance of a small, intimate theater but also provide the opportunity to meet and chat with performers of the arts.

Cultural and Educational Activities

IAHC introduces exciting new events each month; you'll not want to miss any of them. Request to be put on their E-mail list and you'll receive weekly updates. Better yet, become a member; then you won't miss out on any of their offerings, and you'll receive the Heritage Line newsletter, published every three months and crammed with information on events. Inquire about their Irish Studies course for adults offered in conjunction with DePaul University.

Poetry

The Cultural Committee hosts monthly poetry readings open to everyone. Read your favorites or your own writing and enjoy discussions with authors and other poem lovers. Readings are on the second Thursday of the month at 7:00 pm in the Art Gallery, second floor.

In addition, they present the Irish Artists series every other month on a Sunday afternoon. These afternoon sessions provide slide show or video of the works of the featured artists and the story of their lives.

The Cultural Committee also arranges a variety of art exhibits in the second-floor gallery. Call 773/282-7035, x10 or e-mail CULTURALLIAISON@IRISHAMHC.COM.

Language
Na Gaeil: Beginning, intermediate and advanced classes in Irish pronunciation, conversation, and reading. High school and older. Contact Michael McMechan at 773/348-6953.

Music
Academy of Irish Music: Children and adult lessons on a variety of instruments, contact Noel Rice at 847/564-1338 or call IAHC.

Irish Heritage Singers: If you're interested in joining this talented group, call director Mary Grimes at 773/410-2688.

Music Sessions: All musicians and music lovers welcome to join in or listen to a fine set of open-play musicians. Wednesday nights, 7:30 to 9:30. Bring your own beverages.

Dance
Anam Mór Academy: Irish step dancing and céilí classes, hosted dances in the Social center every month. Contact Amy Campbell at 773/205-8557.

McNulty Irish Dance: Children's and adults' step dance lessons. Call 847/775-9807.

Mullane Irish Dance: Step dancing classes for children starting at age four. Call 773/775-9807.

Rince Na Cara Dance: Step dancing classes for children age four and a half to adults. Contact Anne Marie Norton: 630/833-6675.

Spriorad Damhsa Irish Dancers: Performance only. No competition. The group performs jigs, hornpipes, and reels to traditional Irish music. Contact IAHC at 773-282-7035.

Trinity Academy of Irish Dance: Step dancing for children, auditions to join various levels. Call 773/774-5961.

Céilí Dance: Francis O'Neill Céilí Club: Beginning, intermediate, and advanced dancers welcome. Partners not required. Call IAHC.

Set Dancing (Céilí): Instruction and practice in set dancing, a forerunner to square dancing. Call IAHC.

Set Dancing Session: Practice session and several rounds of dances for the more experienced set dancers. Call IAHC.

Children's Center for Cultural Studies

Baby Steps and Suzuki Instrumental
For children from six months to five years old. The Suzuki-Orff approach to music education includes group singing, performing, rhymes, and the use of xylophone, glockenspiel, and other percussive instruments.

Music lessons on a variety of instruments are taught by Noel Rice and others at the Academy of Irish Music. Mr. Rice began the Academy with the desire to create a community of young musicians dedicated to playing and sharing traditional Irish music. Contact Noel Rice at 847/564-1338.

Irish School

Meets on Saturday mornings. Children ages 6 to 16 can participate in lessons on Irish heritage, culture, language and art through drama, storytelling, crafts, and games. Visit their Web site at WWW.IRISHAMHC.COM for their summer schedule.

Summer Art Camp

Five-week program for kids ages 7 to 12. The first three weeks are devoted to kite making and field trips, which include the Art Institute and Millennium Park, the National Museum of Mexican Art, and the Field Museum and Museum Campus. The final two weeks of class, when students take on the Celtic Mythology Literacy Project, will focus on creating artwork and stories.

Storytelling (Seanchai)

IAHC sponsors a summer camp for young people. They'll explore the excitement of theatrical storytelling with workshops in acting, voice, and movement combined with techniques such as designing and building props, sets, and costumes.

Children's Choir

Legacy of Erin Children's Choir is for boys and girls ages 8 to 13. A perfect opportunity to learn and perform Irish music and to make new friends. Contact director Mary Grimes at 773/410-2688 or at IRISHHERITAGESINGERS@IRISHAMHC.COM.

North Side GAA

Gaelic Football and Hurling for men, women and youth. Although not a part of the IAHC, this provides the perfect opportunity to meet Chicago's Irish. The GAA sponsors North Side teams for men's Gaelic football and hurling and ladies' Gaelic football and hurling, along with youth sports. Teams meet at Maryville Academy, 1150 West River Road, Des Plaines. Contact Jane Hynes at 847/696-9290, or visit WWW.CHICAGOCELTICYOUTH.COM. Summer camps are available for youth.

Recreational and Social Activities

Bingo: Wednesday night from 6:30 to 9:30 in the Social Center. Pay per card, play pull-tabs, refreshments available.

Crafts: The Arts and Crafts Nimble Thimbles enjoy quilting, needlepoint, crocheting, etc. in an established workshop.

Golf: An annual golf outing is open to anyone interested in meeting other players attempting to achieve the coveted hole-in-one. Contact Alan Duggan at 312/401-2603 or Maureen O'Looney at 773/286-6866, or contact IAHC.

Shamrock American Club: Social group for adults age 40 and above. Card games, dances, gatherings with refreshments, and group trips. Small fee and annual dues.

Tír na nÓg (Forever Young Seniors): Activity and social group for those 55 and above. Trips, outings, speakers, and many other group activities.

Holidays

Christmas

It's never too early to begin planning holiday activities. You'll want to mark your calendar to join fellow members of the IAHC for the traditional "Holiday Around the World" exhibit. Since 1941 Chicago's Museum of Science and Industry has featured decorated trees representing countries around the globe. The tree is usually set up the first Saturday in November and taken down January 6. You must be a member of the IAHC to participate.

Join in the traditional Irish Mass, followed by an Irish Breakfast in the social center. This event usually occurs on the first Sunday in December. Reservations are a must. After breakfast, plan on doing some holiday shopping. Purchase unique gifts, homemade breads, pies, scones, cakes, and cookies and relax with a "sup" of tea.

The children's choir will entertain you with Christmas carols, and, for an added treat, Santa Claus visits in the early afternoon to meet the children. Inquire about art shows held in the art gallery. Artists are invited to showcase their work, which is also for sale, just in time for holiday gifts.

New Year's Eve

Ring in the new year at the heritage center's Fifth Province Pub. Doors open at 7 pm. Cover charge, hors d'oeuvres, champagne toast at midnight, party favors, dancing and sing along. Authentic Irish music.

St. Patrick's Day

There are not enough hours in the day to celebrate this glorious holiday. Raise your glass to all things Irish and toast your friends with sláinte in the Fifth Province Pub.

Doors open at 12:30 pm just in time for the start of three floors of Irish music, displays, entertainers, dancers, céilí dance lessons, fine foods, and pub-foods. Celebrate with a range of great foods, from sandwiches and breads to a hot buffet prepared and served by some of the best hostesses and Irish cooks in the city and a great pub staff serving the finest in pints and beverages.

I suggest that you call in advance to purchase tickets for the event. They've been known to sell out quickly, and you don't want to miss this opportunity for a day of family fun.

Events

Bloomsday: June 16

On June 16, 1904, writer James Joyce met his wife, Nora Barnacle, and immortalized the date in his monumental epic, *Ulysses*. Modern Joyce aficionados have denoted June 16 as "Bloomsday," a day set aside throughout the world to honor the great man and his controversial and thought-provoking works. Entertainment includes readings and music presented by notables from Chicago's theatre and music community.

Irish Festival

Don't miss this event. Scheduled for three days in July for the past 20 years, it has grown to include music stages and folk tents that house sing-alongs, dances, and demonstrations of Irish instruments. Irish and American food is available, and dozens of vendors and artisans will be selling Irish clothing, music, and jewelry. Don't miss the matchmaking and dancing contests and the mayhem that will surely delight and entertain you The library, museum, and theaters are open for your pleasure. The perfect family day! Call 773/282-7035 for more information.

Samhain Festival

Did you ever wonder how Halloween got its start in America? Why the costumes, candy, and bonfires? The Samhain (SOW-en)celebration marks the beginning of winter and the yearly opening of the Celtic underground. The Celts believed that, on the evening between the last day of fall and the first day or winter, the world went a bit off balance. They believed the souls of the people who died in the previous year would go into the next world. These dead souls could switch with living souls and take their place in the living world. We celebrate this as Halloween and All Saints' Day.

The IAHC celebrates these holidays in the true style of the Irish. They've expanded their exploration of the holiday to include similarities and differences between Celtic Samhain and Mexican Day of the Dead events commemorating one's ancestors. Festivities extend for a month. Call to inquire about what's scheduled.

Volunteering

There are opportunities for young and old to help out nearly every day. Like to bake? The labor crews appreciate baked goods for their daily coffee breaks. Would you like to help repair or build? Tradesmen, handymen, and hobby-helpers are welcome. If you're interested in serving as a docent for the museum and center tours, call the IAHC. Are your archival

skills up to par? The center would appreciate your help sorting through numerous collections of art, music, programs, decorations, books, and other materials. This provides the perfect opportunity for involvement within the Irish community. Contact Tom Boyle at 773/282-0380.

Fifth Province Pub

No place could call itself a total Irish experience without offering a trip to the pub. The in-house Fifth Province offers up the real deal on Friday and Saturday nights, right down to the full selection of Irish beers, the tasty pub grub, and the authentic Irish music sessions. The pub got its name from a remark Irish president Mary Robinson made when she visited the center in 1991. "The Irish in America," she said, "are the country's Fifth Province." Does it get any more Irish than this?

Gaelic Park

Chicago Gaelic Park

6119 West 147th Street, Oak Forest
708/687-9323
www.chicagogaelicpark.org

Located in Oak Forest, Chicago's Gaelic Park is home to one of the most successful Irish athletic, cultural, and recreational facilities in the country. Construction began in 1983 on little more than nine acres. Six more acres were purchased in 1987. Thirty additional acres were leased to provide expanded parking, practice fields, and picnic

Gaelic Park, Oak Forest.

grounds in 1990. Five additional acres were purchased in 1998, bringing the total acreage to 50—ideal for hosting sporting events.

Take in a game of Gaelic football or hurling, cheer your favorite rugby team, visit the pub for traditional Irish music and good craic, and indulge in some tasty pub grub. Join sports fans on Sunday mornings in the Tara Room at 8 am from June to September for the All-Ireland games telecast live from Ireland. Enjoy true Irish hospitality.

Visit their Web site for additional offerings. Become a member and receive their Gaelic Park Newsletter, which details sporting events as well as cultural affairs and other fun activities.

Cultural and Educational Activities

Dancing

Set Dancing: For adults every Monday evening. Instructors provided. Call: 708/598-5313.

Céilí Dancing: Every Tuesday evening. Call: 708/372-6227.

Children's Step Dancing Classes: Call Gaelic Park for details.

Irish Set Dance and Music Weekend: Held in January.

Music
Irish Music Lessons: The Irish School of Music teaches a variety of instruments (tin whistle, flute, fiddle, and more). Contact Sean Cleland at 773/412-6166 or Pat Finnegan at 312/927-2365.

Music Sessions: The Irish Music School hosts a Thursday evening session in the Carraig Pub.

Media
Weekly Radio Station: Tune your radios to WCEV 1450 AM Sundays from 7:05 pm to 9 pm for a wonderful program presented by hosts Mary Riordan, Mary Hackett, or Harry Costelloe. They'll play your favorite tunes and bring you the news direct from Ireland.

Recreational and Social Activities

Ladies Auxiliary: A great ladies night out! Monthly meetings include bingo for prize money and a variety of special events.

Luncheons: Make your reservations early for Gaelic Park's monhly luncheon; there's usually a large crowd. Doors open at noon and lunch is served at 1 pm. Music for dancing continues until 4 pm.

Reflection: Stroll through the grotto dedicated to Ireland's patron saints, Patrick and Bridget. Look for the beautifully sculpted Great Irish Famine Memorial proudly displayed in front of Gaelic Park.

Trivia: Bring a team and come test your knowledge every Tuesday at 8 pm and see if you can stump the quizmaster.

Holidays

New Year's Eve
Celebrate in Irish style in the Tara Room.

St. Patrick's Day
Queen Contest: Annual contest is held two weeks before St. Paddy's Day. Deadline for entry application is Feb. 26. Contact Kay Knightly at 708/422-3503.

Irish Soda Bread Contest: Held the first Sunday in March. Cash prizes.

St. Patrick's Day Parade: A bus leaves Gaelic Park for the downtown St. Paddy's Day Parade. If you'd like to march in Chicago's biggest yearly event for the occasion, contact Gaelic Park for details.

St. Patrick's Day Luncheon: Served at noon. Reservations are a must. Call to reserve your tickets.

St. Patrick's Day Dinner and Concert: Begins at 6 PM, dinner served at 7. Call to reserve tickets.

Events

Sunday Events
Mass and Authentic Irish Breakfast: Second Sunday of every month from October through May. The Gaelic Park Choir performs at the monthly Mass and for special occasions.

Celtic Supper: Live entertainment and dancing every Sunday night from the first Sunday in October through May in the Emerald Room. A full-time Chef prepares the scrumptious meals that are fit for an Irish king.

Annual Events
Irish Festival: Runs Memorial-Day weekend. Join the thousands who gather to listen to traditional and contemporary Irish music, Irish theater, and storytelling. You'll find contests, Irish step dancers, céilí dancing, an Irish dog breeders exhibit, a bonnie baby contest, a red hair and freckles contest, puppet shows, magicians, and much more family fun. See the Irish Festivals/Events chapter in this book for additional information.

Heritage and Harvest Day: Held annually. Call for date and time.

Carraig Spring Charity Walk: Contact the park at CHICAGOGAELIC-PARK@SBCGLOBAL.NET for more information.

Carraig Pub: Visit the Carraig Pub (Irish for "the Rock") to view live sports telecasts from Ireland on Saturdays and Sundays (an Irish breakfast will be available only at the All-Ireland Hurling and All-Ireland Football games). Games of hurling, Gaelic football, and rugby are televised throughout the day. Cheer your favorite teams; watch all televised sports (American games as well as Ireland and England) while enjoying a thirst-quenching brew. The pub, constructed with materials and workmanship direct from Ireland, offers a cozy fireplace and authentic Irish atmosphere. Open to the public from 3 pm to 1:30 am, with live entertainment on Friday and Saturday. Traditional Irish fare is served throughout the day, including a fish fry or a chicken in the basket dinner every Friday. Take time to look over the 33 hand-carved and painted oak plaques from Ireland that hang in the entrance hallway. Thirty-two plaques represent the counties of Ireland, with an additional plaque for the present home of many Irish — County Cook, Illinois.

Come for the good food, and join their traditional Irish music session every Thursday evening, when you'll hear tunes performed by members of the Irish Musicians Association. The Carraig serves the best Guinness on the South Side and carries all the other Irish favorites.

And speaking of Guinness, every Tuesday in February comes the Keep the Glass Program, with historic Guinness labels reminding us of the history and heritage of Guinness.

Banquet Facilities: Whether it's a hooley you're planning or a more formal affair, banquet facilities can be rented for a day or an evening. The Emerald Room and the Tara Room both fit approximately 500 people. Three smaller meeting rooms accommodate between 30 and 125 people. Plan your next event at Gaelic Park; you'll be impressed with its lovely ambiance and charming appearance. Various groups also host many fashion shows and expos at these facilities.

Education,
Language,
and Media

Saint Xavier University, Chicago.

If you live in the Chicago area, you've no doubt laid claim to a favorite Irish pub, and you know where to find the parade on St. Paddy's Day. "Erin Go Braugh" rolls off the tongue along with "Top of the Mornin'," and emerald-colored cookies delight your taste buds. These lighthearted, carefree traditions capture everyone's attention on March 17. For one day each year it's everything Irish, but what about the other days?

There exists an Irish culture some folks don't know about. It's not something you pour into a shot glass or a pint, and it's not funny hats blinking green; rather, it's thousands of years of poetry, history, and legend. Famous writers like James Joyce, William Butler Yeats, George Bernard Shaw, and Samuel Beckett have excelled in fiction, poetry, and drama. Works from Ireland's playwrights, novelists, short story writers, poets, historians, humorists, and philosophers continue to hold their place in the front ranks of world literature. We're not just talking about the gift of gab here but about pure genius.

The many benchmarks of Ireland's fascinating history have made a major impact on the world: the Middle Stone Age period (10,000 bc), the arrival of the Celts (600 bc), St. Patrick's Christian influence (ad 432), the beginning of the 800-year struggle between English and Irish (1167), the Anti-Catholic laws (1695), the Potato Famine (1845–49), and the Irish Civil War (1922).

Considering Ireland's history of political turmoil, one can only wonder how the Irish culture has survived at all. Taking into account the continuing conflicts between south and north, Ireland has evolved from a backward country, one of the poorest in Europe, to one of the fastest-growing economies in Europe.

Chicago's most prestigious universities and colleges support the study of Irish history and culture. Study-abroad programs offer the experience to live and attend school in the large cities of Ireland. Universities in Dublin, Galway, and Limerick invite you to live and study in some of the most culturally diverse cities in the world. This immersion into the Irish lifestyle enhances the experience of Irish culture and tradition.

Ever wondered how your rural Irish ancestors lived? Interested in searching for artifacts? Digging for fossils? How about learning the basics in historical archaeology? If this is something you've considered, then you'll want to travel to the breathtaking county of Donegal to participate in field-study programs. You'll not only earn credit towards a degree but you'll also visit some of the world's most picturesque scenery.

Study-abroad programs provide the opportunity for students to live with Irish families, listen to informative lectures by esteemed Irish scholars, and enjoy the company of professors who are experts in Ireland.

There are also Irish studies programs based here in Chicago whose curricula include Irish history, literature, politics, media studies, culture, language, and more. Check out our neighbors to the north: the University of Wisconsin–Milwaukee offers a fantastic study-abroad opportunity. And let's not forget our Indiana neighbors; the University of Notre Dame hosts amazing educational opportunities at home as well as abroad.

For those who prefer to learn at their own pace, consider Chicago's Newberry

Library. They offer noncredit Irish-themed seminars for people who enjoy learning in small classes.

There's even a fellowship offered at the National University of Ireland in Galway and the opportunity for high school students to explore the rich culture of Ireland. Check out the scholarships listed.

To quote one of Ireland's most famous poets, W.B. Yeats, "Education is not the filling of a bucket, but the lighting of a fire." Just be sure to keep that flame away from Mrs. O'Leary's cow.

You might want to check the American Conference for Irish Studies Web site, WWW.ACISWEB.COM. Their Electronic Guide to Irish Studies in the United States has attempted to list the full range of Irish studies courses being taught in the United States, including classes in literature, history, the social sciences, the arts, the Irish language, and Celtic studies. Although not complete, this guide is a good resource.

Irish Educational Opportunities: Light Your Fire!

Colleges, Universities, and Libraries

Credit and non-credit classes are included below. Offerings are subject to changes. A school or program's Web site is the best source for current information.

DePaul University

Irish Studies Program, 773/687-1000

2320 North Kenmore Avenue

Dr. James Murphy (director)

773/325-4859

www.depaul.edu

DePaul offers a minor in Irish Studies. All course work can be completed on their Chicago campus. The College of Liberal Arts and Sciences offers a study-abroad program in Dublin twice each year. It provides an excellent opportunity for students to get to know Ireland firsthand. Contact Dr. James Murphy for additional information.

Illinois State University

International Studies and Programs

Campus Box 6120, Normal

309/438-5365

Jimmy Brazelton

jebraze@ilstu.edu,
Internationalstudies@ilstu.edu/

Illinois State offers a study-abroad program for undergraduate and graduate students interested in studying in Ireland. A full-year program is offered at the University of Limerick. There are two summer programs available: a three-week program at the University of Limerick and a four-week historical archaeology program in the beautiful Glenveagh National Park in County Donegal. Excavations have taken place on tenant village sites in north County Roscommon as well as in County Sligo. This program is the first anthropologically based project of its kind in Ireland that specifically concentrates on the archaeology of the seventeenth through nineteenth centuries. In earlier years, students have collected over 12,000 artifacts, which include smoking pipes, glass beads, thimbles, pieces of Irish-made and imported English ceramics, and numerous other objects once used every day in rural Irish homes. Contact the Centre for the Study of Rural Ireland, Campus Box 4660, Illinois State University, CEORSER@ILSTU.EDU, or Charles E. Orser, Distinguished Professor of Anthropology, 309/438-2271, Web site: WWW.ILSTU.EDU/~CEORSER/.

Illinois State University - Dr. Orser's students discover relics in Ireland.

Loyola University

6525 North Sheridan Road
773/508-2227
Janet Nolan
jnolan@luc.edu.

Loyola offers undergraduate and graduate courses in modern Irish and Irish American history within the European or American history degree programs. Loyola's reciprocal exchange program in Limerick (offered through Mary Immaculate College Exchange Program) offers a cost-effective opportunity for undergraduates who are willing to accept the challenges of a highly independent study-abroad program. Contact the program at 773/508-7706 or INTLCNTR@LUC.EDU.

Newberry Library

60 West Walton Street
312/255-3665
Rachel Bohlman
bohlmannr@newberry.org.
www.newberry.org

If you find yourself overwhelmed by the length and difficulty of *Ulysses*, you're not alone. Sign up for the Newberry's seminar on James Joyce's famous novel. Study the beauty of the book's organization and the good old-fashioned story-telling pleasure the book offers. If you're thinking of delving into family genealogy, check out the Newberry's informative seminars, and become familiar with their new databases that focus on Irish research. Check their catalog for any upcoming Irish literature seminars that might be scheduled. Visit their Web site for details.

Northern Illinois University

Weston Hall 215, DeKalb, Illinois
815/753-6989
Jeffrey Chown
jchown@niu.edu.
www.niu.edu

Northern Illinois University - Dr. Chown with his students in Ireland.

Northern offers a four-week study-abroad program at Dublin City University. The program is open to individuals who have an interest in the areas of communication, media studies, literature, and film. Currently enrolled students must meet NIU Graduate School or College of Liberate Arts and Sciences GPA requirements. For undergraduate students to be admitted to the program, an applicant's official transcript must be on file in the study-abroad office. Students lodge with Irish families in Dublin and at a youth hostel when they travel to the music festival in Galway. The age range for this program spans from 20 to 70.

Expect the unexpected while in Dublin; you never know what you'll encounter. A few students found themselves at Bono's U2 studio in Dublin. When Bono arrived in his limousine, he graciously offered the students a tour of his studio. Talk about worth the price of that ticket to Ireland! Another time, an Irish director filming the movie *In America* enlisted Dr. Chown's students for one of the pub scenes. It was easier for the director to use Americans in an Irish pub than to fly to New York to film. Unfortunately, Dr. Chown wasn't able to work this gig into the student's schedule.

Northwestern University

Study-Abroad Office
630/Dartmouth Place, Evanston
847/467-6400
www.northwestern.edu/studyabroad

Northwestern offers a study-abroad program at University College Cork. This program is sponsored by the Center for Education Abroad (Arcadia University). Northwestern University students register at Arcadia and receive Northwestern class credits.

Roosevelt University

430 South Michigan Avenue
312/341-3723
Ellen O'Brien
eobrien@roosevelt.edu
www.roosevelt.edu

Roosevelt offers a class in contemporary Irish women's writing and the politics of gender. In this course, you will examine poetry, drama, novels, and short stories written by Irish women between 1960 and the present. Particular attention is paid to the ways in which writers represent and challenge Irish paradigms of gender in various contexts—particularly those constituted by domestic politics, sexual codes, religious mandates, and national/nationalist discourses. Authors will include Edna O'Brien, Molly Keane, Medbh McGuckian, Nuala ní Dhomhnaill, Eavan Boland, Eiléan Ní Chuilleanáin, Emma Donoghue, Mary Dorcey, Patricia Burke Brogan, Anne Devlin, and Marina Carr.

Saint Mary's

Notre Dame, Indiana
800/551-7621
www.stmarys.edu

Offers a course on the history of Ireland. Independent study is available; work with a professor on a project of Irish study. Their study-abroad program in Ireland is offered for one year or one semester.

Saint Xavier University

School for Continuing and Professional Studies, Irish Studies Program
18230 Orland Parkway, Orland Park
708/802-6200
Barbara Walder
walder@sxu.edu.
www.sxu.edu/cps/irish.studies/asp

This Irish Studies program is offered for non-credit. Students can choose from Modern Irish History, Gaelic Lanuguage, Irish Women Writers and/or Researching Your Irish Roots. Classes meet at the Orland Park campus. Each course requires an average of 15 to 20 hours of instruction. Visit their Web site to access their online registration form.

They also offer a Saturday Irish Studies Summer Program called Celts to Christians: Ireland in Late Antiquity and the Early Middle Ages.

Southern Illinois University

Department of English, Irish and Irish-Immigration Studies
Carbondale
618/453-6851
www.lib.siu.edu/~ireland/
Charles Fanning, director
celtic42@siu.edu

Southern Illinois University offers a graduate program with Irish studies as a major or minor field of study. You'll find Irish literature and film as well as Irish language listed in their catalog. SIU also offers a study-abroad program in Galway for Graduate students.

The Graduate Program in Irish and Irish Immigration Studies at SIUC is expanding. There is an active student organization, The Irish Studies Forum meets regularly on an informal basis to discuss topics in Irish and Irish immigration studies, as well as the members' own projects. Each year, the Irish studies program sponsors readings and visits from prominent writers and scholars in Irish studies.

University of Chicago

Harper 213
1116 East 59th St.
773/702-8615
Lewis Fortner, director of study abroad
fortner@uchicago.edu

Complete a year of academic study at Trinity College in Dublin, Ireland, the center of intellectual exploration. In order to be eligible for the program, you must be enrolled as student in the U of C undergraduate program and be in good standing. If you're an adventurous soul looking to truly experience this ancient city, take advantage of the opportunity to live off-campus; what better way to meet the Irish who live and work in Dublin. Applications are available and are to be submitted online, but before applying, students are urged to discuss their plans with their college advisor and consult a study abroad advisor.

University of Illinois at Springfield

One University Plaza, MS HRB 52
Springfield
217/206-6678
www.uis.edu

The University of Illinois offers a Global Experience Program at Trinity College in Dublin. Trinity has agreed to accept qualified UIS students for a semester or year of study. Students can apply either directly to Trinity College or through the University of Illinois–Springfield. College credit will be issued from Trinity College.

University of Notre Dame

South Bend, Indiana
www.nd.edu

Even though admission to the University is highly competitive, with five applications for each freshman class position, don't let this discourage you. Notre Dame offers one of the finest Irish Studies programs in the country. Their Keough-Naughton Institute for Irish

Studies provides undergraduate programs in the Irish literature and language. Graduate programs are also available. If your goal is to pursue higher education in Ireland, their study abroad program offers many opportunities through their Dublin-based program.

University of Wisconsin–Milwaukee

Center for Celtic Studies
Holton Hall 290, P.O. Box 413
Milwaukee, Wisconsin
414/229-2608
www.uwm.edu/Dept/celtic/

Enroll in the Irish language and culture studies classes held at UW's Milwaukee campus. Discover Irish language and culture with classes in folklore, archaeology, tin whistle, bodhrán, fiddle, art, and pottery. Live in a welcoming Donegal coastal community noted for its lively music traditions. Check their Web site, WWW.UWM.EDU/DEPT/CELTIC/SPEAKRS.HTML, for the many events scheduled throughout the year. For an updated course schedule go to WWW.UWM.EDU/SCHEDULE.

Educational Scholarships

IES Abroad

33 North LaSalle Street, 15th Floor
800/995-2300
www.IESabroad.org

The John Gearen Endowed Scholarship Program is available for students who meet the criteria of an acceptable grade point average and approval from their university or college of attendance to participate in the IES Dublin program. This scholarship can be worth up to $3,000 per semester. Applicants must attend the IES Dublin program. Students on the IES Dublin program may be eligible to take one or more courses at one of several colleges and universities in Dublin. A complete list of scholarship requirements can be found on the IES Web site.

U.S.–Ireland Alliance

2800 Clarendon Boulevard.,
Suite 502
West Arlington, Virginia
http://www.us-irelandalliance.org/
mitchellscholarships

The Mitchell Scholarship supports one year of graduate study in any discipline offered by an institution of higher learning in Ireland and Northern Ireland. Applications must be submitted electronically through their Web site. You must show a credible record of accomplishment in leadership and service, as well as academic excellence. Ethnic origin or ancestry is not a factor in the selection process; they welcome and encourage candidates of all ethnic, racial, religious, and political to apply. You must show proof of U.S. citizenship.

Irishman Garrett Kelleher, who is building the world's tallest residential building in Chicago, was recently honored for his commitment of $1 million to the U.S.-Ireland Alliance. The contribution will be matched by the Irish Government to assure the permanence of this scholarship. The scholarship program welcomes applicants of all backgrounds, regardless of race, color, religion, gender, sexual orientation, physical handicap, or political affiliation. All applications must be submitted online.

Incorporated Society of Irish/American Lawyers

c/o Thomas F. Myers, Esq.
1000 Woodbridge Place
Detroit, Michigan 48207-3192
http://www.home.earthlink.net/~isial/id
12.html

Each year the Incorporated Society of Irish/American Lawyers awards two $1,500 scholarships to second or third year law students. Applicants will be asked to provide their resume, financial need, transcripts, and a short letter stating why they should be awarded the scholarship.

Saint Xavier University, John T. & Elizabeth Downs Cartan Scholarship

Chicago Campus: 3700 West 103rd Street
773/298-3000
Orland Park Campus: 18230 Orland Parkway
708/802-6200

The award is need-based, and consideration will be given to a student from the Republic of Ireland. In the event that there are not any Irish student applicants, then this scholarship will be awarded to an American student of Irish decent from Cook County, Illinois.

Fellowships

Irish American Cultural Institute/National University of Ireland Fellowship

773/238-7150
info@iaci-usa.org

Granted to an Irish Studies scholar, this fellowship provides a $13,000 stipend, plus transatlantic transportation, office accommodations, and visiting faculty status at the University of Ireland-Galway. You must be a resident of the United States in order to apply. Visit their Web site for details.

U.S.-Ireland Alliance

The U.S.-Ireland Alliance (see above) offers The George J. Mitchell Fellowship.

Check with the dean of students at your school for additional information.

Cultural Experiences for Teenagers

Irish Way Program

773/238-7150, 973/605-1991
www.iaci-usa.org

The Irish American Cultural Institute sponsors a summer program abroad for American high school students. This is an opportunity for young people to explore the rich heritage and tradition of Ireland, while experiencing the country's distinct culture. Based in Galway, students have the opportunity to explore the west coast of Ireland, travel to Dublin to visit the world-renowned Abbey Theatre, and attend Gaelic football and hurling games. Structured classes consist of Irish language, literature, and history, as well as cultural workshops. Students are responsible for all costs. Visit their Web site for details.

Irish Language: From the Irish Sort of English to the Real Deal

Hiberno-English

Even though the Irish speak English, you might not understand what is being said—it takes some getting used to, because it's an Irish sort of English. Listen with a careful ear; unless you're familiar with the vocabulary and pronunciation, you'll be left out in the cold for much of the conversation.

Irish folks just say things differently and with varying accents. It doesn't help that there are 32 counties in Ireland with different regional dialects. When conversing with my cousins from County Roscommon, I have a devil of a time. One-on-one, I do okay. But with all of the lads, I'm easily lost. They might say, "He's after going to the shops," and by the time I've figured that out, they've moved on to other topics. My cousins in County Kerry are a bit easier to understand, but then there's that unfamiliar word or two that takes me out of the loop—always the Yank!

You'll do well to learn some of the lingo along with a few phrases to slip into your conversation. For instance, if an Irishman greets you with, "An'ting strange?" You'll answer, "Divil a bit!" or "I'm spot on!" Reference to the weather might bring, "Twould skin ye!" Health is a great topic of discussion, and you might hear someone describe a friend's condition as, "He'll soon be a load for four!" or, "I've a *meadhrán* in me head!" If you're telling some astonishing tales, you might hear the response, "Go 'way out o' that!" or "You're havin' me on!" Most recently I greeted an Irishman with, "You're looking grand!" He responded with, "'Tis the divil pulling me leg!"

Once you're comfortable with the vocabulary and phrasing, you'll need to master the lyrical sound. Rent Irish films such as *Waking Ned Divine* or *Darby O'Gill and the Little People*; these movies portray Irish culture in a humorous and affectionate manner, and you'll hear the accent. Rehearse the inflection by repeating lines from the movie into a tape

recorder. Repetition will serve you well; it's the practice you'll need in order to perfect the skill of delivery. Avoid phrases such as "begorrah," "blarney," and "top of the mornin'" because they are not typically Irish expressions. The English coined the term bróg, meaning "shoe," so it's best to refer to the Irish as having an accent rather than a bróg.

If it's truly the immersion of the real Irish language you're looking for, then enroll in an Irish language course and experience the rich culture of Irish through the medium of its own language. Become a part of an elite group with access to a vibrant and brilliant body of literature written in the language of your ancestors.

Modern Irish Language

The Irish language is often referred to as Gaelic or Irish Gaelic, but in Ireland it's called the Irish language or simply Irish. The use of the term Irish avoids confusion with Scottish Gaelic, the closely related language spoken in Scotland and referred to in English as Gaelic.

One of the oldest languages in Europe, Irish was most widely spoken in Ireland until the nineteenth century. Deemed illegal during British rule and nearly obliterated before and during the time of the Great Famine of 1847, the language survives. Even as recently as the 1970s, residents in the large cities of Ireland were critical of their own language, prohibiting their children from speaking it and encouraging instead the use of English. Irish represented the badge of the rural, the backward, and the culturally repressed.

Today, Irish is experiencing a major renaissance, and more people are able to speak and write it than ever before. Not only is the Irish language recognized as the first official language of Ireland, it's also an official language of the European Union. Irish is a required course taught to every student enrolled in the National Schools of Ireland, and street signs in the Republic of Ireland display Irish with English translations.

The language is not difficult to learn but requires repetition, practice, and an ear for pronunciation. The alphabet in Irish is the same as in English, but sometimes you'll see vowels with a mark over them—this is called a fada (FAH-da) or long sign, as in "Sláinte!" (SLAWN-cha) The fada completely changes the pronunciation of vowels, making them longer: *á* is pronounced AW, *é* like the long *a* in "pay," and *ó* and *ú* like the long *o* in "home" and the *oo* in "too." The consonant s is pronounced "sh" before *e* or *I*, as in "Seán" (SHAWN). The double-letter combinations *dh*, *fh*, and *gh* are usually silent; for example, "Laoghaire" is pronounced like the English word "leary." "Hello" in Irish is "dia dhuit" (JEE-uh ghuitch), which literally translates to "God with you." You reply with, "Diás Muire dhuit" (JEE-us MWIR-eh ghuitch), which means "God and Mary with you." "Thank you" in Irish is "Go raibh maith agat" (guh ruh MAH uh-gut).

If you're passionate about learning to speak the Irish, contact the schools listed. Courses are offered at many fine universities as well as at the Irish American Heritage Center in Chicago. Internet sites cater to those who prefer to study at their own pace. There is even a meet-and-chat group for those eager to practice what they've learned with others from the Chicago area.

Modern Irish Language Schools

Irish American Heritage Center

4626 North Knox Avenue
773/282-7035
www.irishamhc.com

Beginning, intermediate, advanced classes in Irish pronunciation, conversation, and reading. Classes meet on Wednesday evenings and Saturday mornings. Contact Michael McMechan or Kelly Shea Doherty through the IAHC. Classes organized by Na Gaeil, independent nonprofit organization based at IAHC.

Teaching strategies include engaging students in conversation. Some instructors may take excerpts from dual-language short stories and work with students on the literal translation of the text. Reading contemporary writing as well as traditional Irish literature teaches an appreciation for the Irish language and culture.

Irish language books, Irish American Heritage Center's library.

St. Xavier University

18230 Orland Parkway, Orland Park

708/802-6200

www.sxu.edu/cps/irish_studies.asp

Barbara Walder, 708/633-4711

walder@sxu.edu

An introduction to the Irish language through use of literature, music, sports, and history. Emphasis is placed on functional Irish words that are commonly used. Class presents an exploratory look at the progression of the language through time. Evening classes.

University of Notre Dame

Department of Irish Language and Literature

422 Flanner Hall

Notre Dame, Indiana 46556

574/631-3555

irll@nd.edu

The Keough Institute for Irish Studies at the university has seen a phenomenal growth of students taking Irish classes since 1992. In 2004 the department of Irish language and literature officially opened. They've also just recently made available their unrivalled Irish-language collection in the Hesburgh Library. Contact them for additional information.

University of Wisconsin–Milwaukee

Center for Celtic Studies

Holton Hall 290, P.O. Box 413

Milwaukee, Wisconsin

414/229-2608

www.uwm.edu/Dept/celtic/

UWM's program was the first outside of Ireland to receive funding from the Irish government to develop programs in the Irish language and culture and has since become a model for other similar programs. Look for their major exhibit on Celtic culture, inspired by the Book of Kells. Contact John Gleeson at the above address for additional information.

Irish Language on the Internet

Daltaí na Gaeilge

www.daltai.com

Offers programs to promote and teach the Irish language. You'll find discussion forums, Irish grammar, phrases, proverbs, games, news, events, articles, and short stories, as well as places to learn the Irish language.

The Chicago Irish Language Meetup Group

http://irish.meetup.com/112

Internet site to meet and speak with people in Chicago who wish to improve their ability to speak, read, and write in Irish, as well as share an appreciation for the Irish culture.

Irish Lessons

www.maths.tcd.ie/gaeilge/lessons.html

Vocabulary and Grammar lessons taken from *Learning Irish* by Micháel ó Siadhail, published by Yale University Press, 1988.

Irish Phrases

www.freepages.genealogy.rootsweb.com/
irelandlist/phrases.html

Irish Language Scholarship

Daltaí na Gaeilge

www.daltai.com

If you're a teacher or prospective teacher, you might be interested in their scholarships, which are offered to those interested in continuing Irish Language studies in Ireland. If you're not able to travel to the ould sod, then take a look at their weeklong Irish Immersion Program held every summer in upstate New York. Visit their Web site for details.

Irish Media: Just the Facts!

A good source of information on all the latest Irish news and events is right here under your nose. With radio shows, TV, newspapers, magazines, and newsletters, Chicago's Irish media covers local, national, and international issues.

Children's Irish language book, Irish American Heritage Center library.

Become a member of the Irish American Heritage Center and receive their quarterly newsletter. You'll be informed of the cultural, educational, theatrical, and literary events that go on every day at the center. Gaelic Park puts out a similar quarterly newsletter listing their activities, along with all the Irish sporting events held at the park. These quarterlies also print newsworthy accounts for the Irish community.

Subscribe to the Irish American News for information on sporting events, traditional and contemporary music, festivals, and just about everything else concerning the Irish in Chicago. There are also informative columns from enlightened and entertaining journalists. Some broadcasts and news journals are available on the Internet.

Local Radio

WPNA 1490 AM

408 South Oak Park Avenue, Oak Park

773/638-8888, 708/524-9762

www.wpa1490am.com

Bud Sullivan: Saturday morning, 8 to 9 am

The Hagerty Family Irish Hour: Saturday morning, 9 to 11 am

Tune in and catch one of Chicago's most listened to radio shows. You'll not only hear good Irish music but also the latest news on what's happening in and around the Irish community.

Mike O'Connor Show: Saturday, 11 am to 1 pm

Don't miss this informative two-hour show. You'll hear interviews with some of Chicago's elite politicians, plus the old music of Ireland, featuring lively jigs and reels.

WCEV 1450 AM

5356 West Belmont Avenue

773/282-6700

www.wcev1450am.com

Good Morning Ireland with Sean Ginnelly: Saturday, 1:05 to 3 pm

224/715-8292

www.goodmorningireland.net

Set your dial to 1450 AM for all the latest news and sports from Ireland, along with lively interviews, good music, and a bit of playful humor thrown in for good measure. Sean Ginnelly, born and raised in Castlebar, County Mayo, hosts this informative, upbeat show with such enthusiasm you'll

not want to touch the dial. Tune in to hear Eileen Magnier's informative and engaging news reports. Eileen is the northwestern correspondent for Ireland's national broadcaster RTE. For all the latest breaking news and up-to-the-minute sports news in Ireland, go to WWW.RTE.IE.

Gaelic Park Irish Hour with Mary Riordan, Mary Hackett and Harry Costello: Live broadcast from Gaelic Park on Sunday, 7 to 9 pm

708/687-9323

www.chicagogaelicpark.org

Hear Irish tunes and news direct from Ireland. Enjoy entertaining, good-natured banter.

WDCB 90.9 FM

College of DuPage

425 Fawell Boulevard, Glen Ellyn

630/942-9322

www.cod.edu/wdcb/

Blarney on the Air with Shay Clarke and Bill Margeson: Monday, 7 to 9 pm

SHAYDUB@AMERITECH.NET, WWW.WDCB.ORG

Guaranteed to entertain, Shay and Bill host the best of Celtic music, old and new, contemporary and traditional. Each two-hour program is full of fascinating facts about Celtic music, as well as stories and inside information about Ireland. They discuss everything from Irish weather to their favorite sports in Ireland.

Look for monthly columns in the *Irish American News* by Shay ("Raised on Songs and Stories") and Bill ("Tradition in Review"). They'll keep you informed of recently released CDs, music venues, events, and festivals that you won't want to miss. You can find these newspapers at all the Irish establishments throughout

Shay Clarke and Bill Margeson on the air.

the city and suburbs, or subscribe and have them delivered to your door. Call Ian at 708/445-0700.

WHPK 88.5 FM

5706 South University Avenue
773/702-8289
www.whpk.org

A Feast of Irish Folk with Mary Caraway: Monday, 5 to 6:30 pm
Tune in to hear wonderful Irish tunes, from the latest releases to the compositions of traditional masters.

WSBC 1240 AM

Access Radio
5626 North Milwaukee Avenue
773/792-1121, 773/286-6866

Maureen O'Looney Show: Wednesday, 9 to 10 pm
Irish music and interesting talk fill the airwaves. Join Maureen for an hour of good entertainment.

Radio from Ireland

The Craic
www.getthecraic.com

An exclusive online radio show from Dublin for the Irish abroad, wherever they live and whatever their generation. Presenter Ian Dempsey makes it all very cozy with a lively 30-minute show full of stories and information on music, sports, and entertainment, which is more fun than reading a Web site. You can access past interviews at their Web site.

Other Irish Stations:
WWW.MIDWESTIRISHRADIO.COM: News and music.
WWW.FM104.IE: Dublin's hit music station.

Local Television

Irish Journal TV
CAN-TV, Channel 19, Monday 7 pm, Tuesdays, 2 pm
Michael P. Morley (producer), 708/366-4665
IRISHTV@AMERITECH.NET, WWW.CANTV.ORG

Irish Journal TV is a weekly half-hour showcase of Irish music, personalities, and events. The show is cablecast to more than a million homes in the greater Chicago area. Irish TV Journal airs primetime on noncommercial channels in all cable systems. Mike also writes a monthly column for the *Irish American News* in Chicago. Don't miss his political commentaries and juicy stories that mainstream media can't find the time or space to cover.

Out of Ireland

WYCC, Channel 20, Wednesday,
6:30 pm, Thursday, 12:30 am

6259 South Union Avenue
773/838-7878

WWW.WYCC.TV

Tune in for news, culture, and entertainment programs presenting the best of modern Ireland. Produced and hosted by Dublin-born journalist Patricia O'Reilly.

Local Newspapers, Magazines, and Newsletters

The American Irish Media Group consists of 10 newspapers coast-to-coast, including Chicago's *Irish American News*. Each paper is individually owned, chooses its own editorials, and operates independently within the group. The main focus is on local, national, and international news of interest to those of Irish heritage, including current events, special events, radio, sports, book reviews, travel, entertainment, poetry, history, calendars of events, classified ads, and features by Irish writers. Visit WWW.AMERICANIRISHMEDIA.COM to view member publications.

Irish magazines, newspapers, publications.

Irish American News

7115 West North Avenue, Oak Park
708/445-0700
www.irishamericannews.com

If you're not already subscribing to Chicago's Irish American newspaper, this is your opportunity to pick up the telephone or visit their Web site to join the long list of Irish and Irish American subscribers who are kept up to date on all things Irish in Chicago and throughout the world. With a distribution of over 25,000 monthly newspapers, they cover music, festivals, events, book reviews, theater, legal questions, sports, trivia, investments, and much more. Chock full of information, this will be your source for Irish happenings in the city. This entertaining, informative newspaper will become a household fixture. If you're thinking of holidays or family events, a subscription to this fine newspaper makes the perfect gift.

The Heritage Line

Irish American Heritage Center
4626 North Knox Avenue
773/282-7035
www.irishamhc.com

This informative quarterly newsletter is one of the perks of becoming a member of the Irish American Heritage Center. It informs members of every event sponsored by the center. You'll be amazed at the wide range of activities available in addition to their regularly scheduled events. Call them today and begin to receive your quarterly newsletter.

Chicago Gaelic Park

6119 West 147th Street, Oak Forest

708/687-9323

www.chicagogaelicpark.com

Become a member of the Irish community at Gaelic Park and receive their quarterly newsletter. Be in the know regarding current updates on all the GAA games, dances, theater performances, parades, events, pub happenings, and much more. Call them, request membership information, and get on their mailing list.

Irish Magazines

Irish America

432 Park Avenue South

New York, NY

212/725-2993

www.irishabroad.com

This magazine circulates throughout the Irish community in the United States and features full-color spreads of Irish events in the U.S. Book reviews and theater news keep you abreast of what's coming to Chicago.

Ireland of the Welcomes

Dublin, Ireland

www.irelandofthewelcomes.com

First published in 1952, this magazine portrays the best of Ireland's history, culture, and lifestyles to many people worldwide. Some of their readers are Irish-born, some have Irish roots, and others simply enjoy reading about the country they are planning to visit.

Web News from Ireland

WWW.IRISHABROAD.COM: Irish news and social networking Web site for Irish expats, descendants, and any person wishing to travel to Ireland.

WWW.IRISHNEWS.COM: News from Ireland. Based in Belfast.

WWW.ONLINENEWSPAPERS.COM: Irish newspapers. For information on Irish issues, politics, events, celebrations, people, and business.

WWW.RTE.IE: The latest Irish, world, and international news.

WWW.INDEPENDENT.IE: News from Ireland and the world, including sports coverage.

WWW.EGT.IE/MISC/NUACHTAIN.HTML: Irish newspaper online, published in Galway.

WWW.IRISHSITES.COM: Irish job vacancies.

WWW.EMIGRANT.IE: News for the global Irish community, published in Galway.

Sports

St. Brendan's Football Club, Chicago.

The GAA officially began in January 1885 at a time when Ireland suffered economic depression under British rule. Penal Laws and decrees were crushing the essential pastimes of hurling, Gaelic football, and athletics. All sporting events in Ireland were under the control of the English Amateur Athletics. All that changed when, in 1882, Michael Cusak, native of Carron, County Clare, showed an interest in reviving Irish games and promoting an Irish Ireland. From humble beginnings, the GAA flourished and grew to become the greatest sporting organization in Ireland.

Gaelic football is increasing in popularity in America. Injuries are minimal, and the action lasts for a full 60 minutes—no time outs, no stoppage for any reasons other than injury, unlike in American football, where the total amount of time the football is actually in play is only about four to five minutes per game.

Hurling has been described as "field hockey in the air," and it exhibits a unique combination of skill, athleticism, stamina, and speed that few sports can match. It's the fastest game on earth and has the speed and continuous flowing action of ice hockey, but on grass. You won't see padded clothing, spiked shoes, or face guards on these Irish teams, only their team jerseys identifying them as players.

There are no professional leagues. The only reward is the honor of winning and representing their community. That's what makes the GAA such a unique organization—no corrupting influence of out-of-control players' salaries and transfer markets.

The greatest prize in Irish games? For football it's the Sam McGuire Cup. In hurling it's the Liam McCarthy Cup. These two finals are Ireland's equivalent of the Super Bowl. The most prestigious prizes in Gaelic games are the inter-county All-Ireland Championships. These occasions are huge.

For local games, check out the North American GAA Club Page Web site. If you're interested in watching the All-Ireland Championships on television, the cable channel Setanta Sports is available on pay-per-view on Direct TV, or look for them at your local Irish pub that shows the games.

Chicago is home to both a North Side GAA and a South Side AA. Check out their Web site for additional information. Sign up and get involved in the games and partake in the action-packed excitement.

Irish Sports

Gaelic Athletic Association (GAA): Gaelic Football and Hurling

Sports offered by the GAA:

WWW.NAGAA.ORG: For local club information.

WWW.GAA.IE: For information on the origins of the games.

Gaelic Park Sports

6119 West 147th Street, Oak Forest
708/687-9323
www.ChicagoGaelicPark.org

Gaelic Football: A mixture of soccer and rugby.

Hurling: Similar to hockey, in that it is played with a small ball and a curved wooden stick. It is Europe's oldest field game and one of the fastest field games in the world.

Camogie: Ladies' hurling.

Rugby: Although not a part of the GAA, the South Side Irish Rugby Football Club plays all home games at Gaelic Park. New players are always welcome. Contact Bill Morrison at 773/931-5915. WWW.SOUTH SIDEIRISHRUGBY.COM.

Gaelic Park is a fantastic destination for many reasons, one of them being that it's the perfect location for ball games. Tucked into a country setting and surrounded by lovely old trees and emerald-green fields, this sports facility is home to the local Gaelic Athletic Association. Men's, women's, and children's games of Gaelic football and hurling are held every Sunday during the summer. Gaelic Park has hosted exhibition matches for the All-Ireland Champions in hurling and Gaelic football and the Continental Youth Championships (with over one hundred participating teams). The North American County Board has hosted their finals over Labor Day weekend. Hurling and football teams with both male and female competitors are represented. Take this opportunity to cheer or harass your favorite team. These action-packed games provide toe-curling excitement, along with the opportunity for you to offer admirable advice to the players from the safety of your chair. The playing field bleachers seat approximately 3,000 people.

The GAA sponsors senior men's football teams, junior men's football teams, ladies football teams, senior hurling teams, Camogie teams, and youth sports.

The North Side teams play at Maryville Academy, 1150 North River Road, Des Plaines. The South Side teams play at Gaelic Park.

Did you know that handball and rounders were included in the original GAA charter back in 1885? Handball is

North Side Youth Gaelic Football Team, Chicago.

like racquetball, only played without the rackets, and rounders is a bat-and-ball game similar to baseball. Although not played at Gaelic Park, perhaps interest would create the necessity to form a team.

Remember that, while the champions are always heroes, the losers in Ireland never actually lose. Instead, they are merely victims of circumstance.

South Side Youth Gaelic Football Team, Chicago, Gaelic Park.

Youth Sports: Gaelic Football and Hurling

The kids will love these games; they last only 60 minutes and are fast paced. They provide the opportunity to not only learn the Irish games but also to meet new friends and get some good exercise.

North Side Teams

Jane Hynes, 847/696-9290
www.chicagocelticyouth.com

South Side Teams

Kathy Ramsey, 630/887-8534
www.chicagoyouthgfc.com

For boys and girls ages 5 to 18; all skill levels welcome. Summer sports camps are offered for both North and South Side teams. Call for details.

Other Sports

Sport is serious business because there is pride at stake. While all hope to win, most will admit it's the participation that counts. Whether you're a fan observing from the stands or a player kicking goals, wrestling opponents, wind milling a 28-ounce steel ball down a country road, or competing in boat races—it's all about the game.

I've provided contact information for all the sports highlighted in this chapter. This is by no means a complete list, but it will get you started.

Although not part of the GAA, the games of rugby, soccer and lacrosse have made their way to Chicago's popular sporting events list. Numerous teams throughout the Chicago area participate in these lively games, and it's not uncommon to hear rousing banter from Irish fans who are defending their favorite teams. On a historical note, for the first time in GAA history, Dublin's Croke Park opened to foreign sports following an agreement with the Football Association of Ireland (FAI) and the Irish Rugby Football Union (IRFU) to allow soccer and rugby Internationals to be played at the home of Gaelic football.

Rugby

The Chicago Area Rugby Football Union (CARFU)

www.chicagorugby.com

CARFU offers rugy referee certification at the Center for Health and Fitness at Loyola University Medical Center in Maywood. Certification is required for anyone who referees a U.S. match that can potentially lead to a national championship.

Chicago Women's Rugby Football Club

www.cwrfc.org

Illinois Youth Rugby

www.iyra.org

Soccer

Illinois State Youth Soccer Association

4036 North Pulaski Road
773/283-2800
www.northernillionoissoccerleague.com

Mayor's Cup Youth Soccer Tournament

312/744-3315
www.cityofchicago.org/specialevents

There is plenty of fun at this annual soccer event. Boys and girls ages 5–14 participate in five-on-five play over nearly 40 fields. Free family activities include music, entertainment, sports, games and more.

Professional Soccer Academy

545 Consumers Avenue, Palatine
847/788-5312
www.professionalsocceracademy.com

Chicago Sport and Social Club

www.chicagosportandsocialclub.com

Soccer locations at Lincoln Park, Brads Park, Montrose Turf, and Union Park indoors. The gym is located at 950 West Weed Street (above North Beach Bar) and Mercy Center-Indoor Turf (1101 W. Adams). Seasons: winter, spring, summer, and fall.

South Side Youth Hurling Team, Chicago, Gaelic Park.

United States Adult Soccer Association

Aurora

George Chazaro (deputy director), 224/521-8170

mason32glc@aol.com

Check with your local park districts for a listing of their soccer schedules.

Lacrosse

Modern lacrosse has been around for about 70 years and has flourished at an international level for both men and women.

Chicago-Illinois Chapter

www.uslacrosse.org

Chicago Shamrox: 877/SHAMROX

www.chicagoshamrox.com

New to Chicago, this team has taken the city by storm. Visit their Web site for game information and to sign up for their newsletter.

Lacrosse America for Boys and Men, Girls and Women:

Highland Park, 847/926-0067

Downers Grove, 630/437-5550

Hoffman Estates, 847/926-9872

Lincoln Park Lacrosse Club

www.lplax.com

Tug-of-War

For those interested in forming a tug-of-war team, I've included information about an organization that's willing to get you started. It's a great way to spend an afternoon and will certainly help to keep those muscles tight and lean.

Gaelic Park

6119 West 147th Street, Oak Forest

708/687-9323

www.Chicagogaelicpark.org

High School tug-of-war competition during their Irish festival held on Memorial Day weekend (call Gaelic Park for details).

U.S. Amateur Tug-of-War Association

800/884-6927

www.usatowa.homesstad.com

National organization affiliated with Tug-of-War International Federation. This organization holds world championships for men, women, and youth every two years. Call to organize tournaments in your area.

Wrestling (Youth)

You don't have to be a student at St. Patrick's High School in order to join the team. Give them a call and get started.

Shamrock Wrestling Club

St. Patrick's High School
5900 West Belmont Avenue
847/508-1741
Joe Moore
jmoore@shamrockwrestling.com
www.shamrockwrestling.com

Ages 8–14. St. Patrick's sponsors a grammar school wrestling team with more than 10 area grade schools participating. You don't have to be a student at St. Patrick's to join. All practices are held in the wrestling room at the high school.

Boxing

The Irish Amateur Boxing Association

www.irishboxing.com

For all you boxing fans, check out their Web site for information on the latest in World Boxing Championships, which also double as the first 2008 Olympic qualifying event. If you're interested in women's professional boxing, the IABA held its first-ever women's professional fight. Interested in their Round Robin tournaments or looking for information on boxing events scheduled in Chicago? Visit their Web site for details.

Irish Road Bowling

The game of Irish Road Bowling dates back to the 1600s. One of Ireland's oldest sporting events, it is most popular in the counties of Cork and Armagh. The player throws a tennis-sized steel ball down the road or path, covering a distance of about 200 feet (or shorter, depending on your skill). In terms of scoring, it's similar to golf; whoever covers the course in the least amount of throws is declared the winner. It's an exciting game that's sure to get you fired up. See below for additional information and contact details.

Irish Road Bowling

David Powell, 202/387-1680
www.wvirishroadbowling.com

This sport is similar to fast-pitch softball, except with a running start. It's also like bowling if you had enough room to run 10 or 15 yards. Irish Road Bowling is ideal for young athletes or seniors who are looking to enjoy a scenic walk on a country road combined with an ancient and exciting, but not overly strenuous, sport. While it's easy to learn, it takes time and skill to become as proficient as some of those who have set records.

Irish Road Bowling, McGinnis Pub, Michigan City, Indiana.

There are teams in Boston, New York, and West Virginia. If you're interested, contact David Powell; he'll get you set up with a starter pack of two road bowls, a rules and strategy booklet, road chalk, and a pencil. Or better yet, check out the McGinnis Pub.

McGinnis Pub

227 West 7th Street
Michigan City, Indiana
219/872-8200
www.mcginnispub.com

Start your Sunday morning with a good Irish breakfast of eggs, rashers, bangers, baked tomatoes, fried potatoes, soda bread and brown bread. Wash it down with a Bloody Mary or a pint of Guinness, then sign up for a game of road bowling. Teams meet on a designated road each week for this rousing sporting event. Young and old participate. It not only provides great exercise (from the walking) but it also brings people of all ages together with the common goal of a victory.

Join their Guinness 100-Pint Club. Once you reach 50 pints, you'll receive a special Guinness prize, and downing 100-

Pints gets your name on a plaque for all to admire—your chance at fame.

You'll want to sign up for their annual Pub Tour of Ireland, which takes place in February. Their stops include Bushmills Distillery, as well as one of the oldest Irish distilleries in the world.

Visit their Web site for additional information on all events.

Currach Racing

Traditional Irish rowing began at the time of Julius Caesar in 100 bc. Early Gaelic accounts speak of large ocean sailing vessels roving the North Atlantic. One such account concerns St. Brendan, an Irish monk from the Middle Ages, who wrote of having made a discovery across the Atlantic under sail and oars in a currach. It is believed that St. Brendan discovered American long before Columbus's historic voyage.

Currachs are still used in Ireland in their traditional role as well as in competition. In the United States there are many rowing clubs dedicated to promoting the nautical heritage of Ireland through currach racing.

The North American Currach Association (www.irishrowing.org) was founded in 1982. They sponsor eight clubs located in various cities throughout the U.S. Help to make Chicago the ninth sponsored city on their list.

McGinnis Pub, Michigan City, Indiana.

Ilinois Mathematics and Science Academy (IMSA)

Aurora

Robb Gill, Head Track and Field Coach

kayak@imsa.edu

With currach racing gaining in popularity, Robb felt this was the time to connect his students to the great sport of Irish rowing. With the help of H-2-O Academy, the New Beginnings Fellowship Church of Batavia, and some very good friends, Robb was able to realize his goal. Currently, the currach teams in the U.S. are almost exclusively made up of adults, but Robb hopes to change this and encourages high schools to start their own programs. He looks forward to seeing gigs, whalers, and the old currachs line up side by side to race; friendships will be formed, new rivalries will emerge, and age-old questions about what is the best boat design will continue to be debated. If you're interested in creating a school team, contact Robb.

Irish American Heritage Center

4626 North Knox Avenue,

773/282-7035

Tom, 847/870-7588;
Harry, 630/469-8723

www.irishamhc.com

Although it is not yet an official club, there is momentum from a small number of folks who wish to get a currach racing team launched in Chicago. Milwaukee has given them a currach to use, and they've located a lake to put it in and have a few rowers. If there is anyone interested in joining, call Tom or Harry. Make this event happen in Chicago by throwing support their way. It's great exercise and a terrific opportunity to meet people.

Pubs and Restaurants

Irish Music School session at Grealy's Pub.

Craic refers to all social life, from a day's work to a night in the pub. Ireland is the only place in the world where craic is legal, and all that's necessary are one or two people, interesting conversation, and a generous mix of excitement and fun. Add to that the Irish accent, a pint of stout, or a glass of whiskey for that touch of authenticity.

In order to impress the bar crowd, you'll do well to familiarize yourself with the brew. Begin with a pint of stout (Guinness) and a small one (whiskey). A few drinks will do no harm, but most will agree you won't feel the best after a night on the tear. Stout is known to calm the nerves and clear the head while whiskey straight up goes down like a candlelit procession. Steady your pace and go easy; even the best intentioned will lose the run of themselves—'tis powerful stuff. (Whiskey in Irish is *uisce beatha* ("water of life"; pronounced ISH-ka BA-ha).

Chicago proudly boasts of having over one hundred Irish pubs, and each one of them offers the delightful mix of *craic agus ceol* ("fun and music"). You'll know when you've happened upon a real Irish pub, because you'll be in the company of authentic Irish people enjoying a two-pour Guinness and pints of Harps, Murphy's, Smithwick's, Power's, or Tullamore Drew, along with offerings of Taytos or Crunchies for sale behind the bar. There might even be a fireplace, live, music and good Irish food.

If it's a pub crawl you're planning, take a look at the "Wearin' O' The Green" chapter, where you'll find information on the Chicago History Museum's Pub Crawl. I can't think of a better way to tour Chicago's pubs than fully supervised and with a trolley driver at the controls.

If it's the Guinness you're after, then you'll be interested to know the legendary two-part pour. Be reverent to the pint and serve at 42.8 degrees Fahrenheit. Tilt the glass to 45 degrees, carefully pouring until three quarters full, then let sit. Once the surge has settled, fill the glass to the brim. It takes about 119.5 seconds (according to the Guiness spokespeople) to pour the perfect pint, but it's well worth the wait. A truly skilled bartender, using the tap's spout, will be able to draw a shamrock onto the head during slow pour. This whole piece of theater, the ritual, is important because most people drink their beer with their eyes first. And don't make an eejit of yourself by sipping the head off a pint; it will surely ruin the drink.

Then there's the other account of the two pour—the Angelus. A bell tolls at noon on Irish radio and 6 pm on Irish television to let anyone who's interested know that it might be a good time for a little prayer. Every pub in Ireland pouring Guinness abandons the pour at noon and at 6 pm and resumes after the prayer. Someone took notice of how this wait time affected the look of the drink. The rest is history.

I've listed pubs that provide traditional Irish music sessions, pubs with restaurants and outdoor patios, and those that just serve the satisfying brew along with good craic. If you don't see your favorite Irish pub listed, I apologize for the oversight—so many pubs, so little time. And if *you* spend enough time exchanging good craic with the Irish, you'll soon be talking with a lilt to your voice in no time at all. And who knows? You might just discover your Irish somewhere at the bottom of a Guinness.

Pubs with Authentic Irish Music Sessions

For those who have most recently traveled to Ireland and listened to traditional Irish music sessions (*seisiúns*) from Doolin to Dublin, then you know the energy, the inspiration, the heart and soul of Irish music. Musicians play for the camaraderie—gathering to share stories, tunes, and music—each tune blending to create perfect synergy with their fiddles, pipes, tin whistles, bodhráns, and button accordions. The music is cross-generational, bringing together old and young, from architects to ironworkers, all with the same objective—to play and listen to the Irish reels and jigs. You don't have to travel all the way to Ireland to get your fill; a handful of Chicago's Irish pubs host sessions. Go for the brew and stay for the music. And if you're skilled enough to join in, you're welcome to do so. There's always room for one more musician. I've listed pubs that host traditional Irish music sessions. However, schedules do change, so be sure to phone before you grab your car keys—you don't want to be disappointed.

Chicago: Downtown

Celtic Crossings

751 North Clark Street
312/337-1005
www.celticcrossingschicago.com

Sessions on Sunday from 5 to 9 pm. Most authentic Irish pub in the city. No food, no TVs just good conversation.

Where the Irish meet: Celtic Crossings, Chicago.

Fado

100 West Grand Avenue
312/836-0066
www.fadoirishpub.com

Sessions on Thursday evening. Rugby, soccer, Gaelic games, and American sporting events broadcast, along with a fantasy league and private league. Serves Irish and American food.

Kitty O'Shea's

720 South Michigan Avenue
312/294-6860
www.hilton.com

Sessions on Tuesday evenings. Irish spirits and live music, entertainment nightly. Lunch and dinner served.

Chicago: North Side

Abbey Pub

3420 West Grace Street
773/478-4408
www.abbeypub.com

Sessions on Sunday from 4 to 8 pm. Watch live international sports telecasts: rugby, soccer, Gaelic and all major American sporting events on their 15-foot screens and their 14 monitors throughout the bar. Live music seven nights a week. Serving brunch, lunch, and dinner. Visit their Web site for additional information.

Chief O'Neill's

3471 North Elston Avenue
773/473-5263
www.chiefoneillspub.com

Sessions on Tuesday and Sunday. Pub, restaurant and banquet facility. Traditional Irish breakfast, lunch, and dinner served. The Irish Music School of Chicago under the direction of Sean Cleland kicks off their new Tuesday evening sessions featuring jigs and reels.

Cullen's

3741 North Southport Avenue
773/975-0600
Sessions on Tuesday at 9 pm. Irish breakfast, sidewalk patio seating reminiscent of Temple Bar District of Dublin.

Galway Arms

2442 North Clark Street
773/472-5555
www.galwayarms.com

Sessions on Sunday evening beginning at 9 pm. Irish and American cuisine. Live music every Thursday, Friday, and Saturday night featuring popular local bands. Watch Gaelic football, soccer, Six Nations Rugby, and all the American games on their satellite TVs. The owner and many of the wait staff and bartenders are from Ireland.

The Grafton Pub

4530 North Lincoln Avenue
773/271-9000
www.thegrafton.com

Sessions on Sunday evenings at 5 pm. Best food and drinks in the area. Traditional Irish and American cuisine.

Grealy's

5001 West Lawrence Avenue
773/736-5400
www.grealyspubchicago.com

Sessions on Wednesday nights. Excellent food and comfortable surroundings.

Grealy's Pub, Chicago.

The Hidden Shamrock

2723 North Halsted Street
773/883-0304
www.thehiddenshamrock.com

Sessions on Sunday from 3 to 6 pm. Lincoln Park's oldest Irish pub. Enjoy the best sporting events on one of nine satellite televisions, including the big-screen Traditional Irish food, music, and decor.

The Irish American Heritage Center

4626 North Knox Avenue
773/282-7035
www.irishamhc.com

Sessions on Wednesday at 7 pm (Room 302). Hear Irish music from Irish-born musicians. Put this on your "must do" list because these guys are a disappearing breed of music makers. Born and raised in Ireland, they learned the craft from their fathers and grandfathers.

The Irish Oak

3511 North Clark Street
773/936-6669
www.irishoak.com

Sessions on Wednesday at 8 pm. Full Irish breakfast, big screen TV to view all major seasonal sporting events, food and drink specials.

McNamara's

4328 West Irving Park Road
773/725-1800
www.mcnamaras.com

Sessions on Thursday and Sunday evenings. Serving daily lunch and dinner specials. Enjoy their weekend Irish breakfast menu.

Martyr's

3855 North Lincoln Avenue
773/404-9869
www.martyrslive.com

Sessions on Monday nights. Visit their Web site for other Irish music entertainment.

Chicago: South Side

Lanigan's Irish Pub

3119 West 111th Street
773/233-4004

Sessions on Sunday evenings. Big-screen TVs for sports fans and cozy snugs to enjoy drink and conversation.

Sunday night session at Lanigan's Pub, Chicago.

Lanigan's Pub, a South side favorite.

North Suburbs

Bridie McKenna's

254 Green Bay Road, Highwood
847/432-3311
www.bridiemckennasirishpub.com

Sessions on Tuesday evenings.
Bridie McKenna's adds an authentic Irish touch to this North Shore neighborhood. Bring your fiddle and join in. Not only great music, but also delicious food, a huge beer selection, and good craic.

Celtic Knot Public House

626 Church Street, Evanston
www.celticknotpub.com

Sessions on Tuesday nights. Good pub grub and a variety of entertainment: Irish storytellers, Bluegrass and Roots music.

Nevin's Pub

1450 Sherman Avenue, Evanston
847/869-0450
www.tommynevins.com

Sessions on Sunday at 2:30 pm.
Traditional Irish food, all day Irish breakfast, sidewalk cafe.

Northwest Suburbs

Peggy Kinnane's

8 North Vail Avenue,
Arlington Heights
847/577-7733
www.peggykinnanes.com

Sessions on Thursday nights
Dining area, private party rooms. Vis their Web site for additional informatio

West Suburbs

Ballydoyle

5157 Main Street, Downers Grove
630/969-0600
www.ballydoylepub.com

Sessions on Sunday evening. Trin ity Irish dancers (call for schedule), live bands, appetizers and salads served, ope mic night, party room.

Molly Malone's

7652 West Madison Street,
Forest Park
708/366-8073
www.themollymalones.com

Sessions on Thursday at 8 pm.
Daily menu specials, two fireplaces, extensive beer and wine selection, party rooms.

Irish Times

369 Burlington Avenue, Brookfield
708/485-8787
www.irishtimespubchicago.com

Sessions on Wednesday at 8 pm.
Delicious Irish food, beer garden, party cottage, movie Mondays featuring free popcorn, Tuesday pub quiz, and Thursday jazz night.

Southwest Suburbs

Chicago Street

5 North Chicago Street, Joliet
815/727-7171
www.chicagost.com

Sessions every Monday evening.
If you're looking for a comfortable neighborhood pub, look no further. The friendly staff and wonderful atmosphere help to create an afternoon or evening of pure enjoyment. Excellent food choices including traditional Irish food. Ask for the "Rugger-Bard," a stack of hamburger, cheese, bacon, onions, and mushrooms and served with a pint of Guinness.

Gaelic Park's Carraig Pub

6119 West 147th Street, Oak Forest
708/687-9323
www.chicagogaelicpark.org

Sessions on Thursday nights. Food served Monday thru Saturday, banquet facilities, local GAA games on fields, live sportscasts of Ireland's Gaelic games.

Irish Manor

11501 South Pulaski Road, Alsip
708/388-1772

Sessions every Sunday at 3 pm.
Authentic Irish bacon and cabbage served every Wednesday and Friday, along with the traditional American corned beef and cabbage. Three fireplaces, four flat-screen plasma TVs and a separate enclosed bar area. Irish brown bread and soda bread baked on premises. Open seven days a week.

Keegan's Pub

10618 South Western Avenue, Evergreen Park
773/233-6829
www.keganspub.com

Sessions scheduled for the second Thursday of every month. No food served, four big-screen TVs for viewing sportscasts.

Murphy's Pub

13100 Southwest Highway, Orland Park
708/448-6550
www.paloscountryclub.com

Sessions scheduled on Friday evenings. Situated at the Palos Country Club, Murphy's is a comfortable and elegant place to unwind after a game on the links. Check out their great menu showcasing their premier sandwiches.

Pubs, Restaurants, and Outdoor Patios

Many of Chicago's Irish establishments serve good pub grub, and if the weather cooperates, you can enjoy an afternoon in the shade or an evening of dining under the stars. Music entertainment might include jukebox, live bands, karaoke, and open mic nights. There's even a pub where you can sip your martini while having a manicure, proving the Irish ingenious when it comes to accommodating their customers.

You'll find Irish pubs in every neighborhood in Chicago, as well as in the suburbs. Each one of them seeks to create an atmosphere reminiscent of Ireland. Whether through food, live bands, cozy snug, or quiet conversations at the bar, you're sure to find one that suits your style. I've provided a listing of some offerings in the area. Pick your favorites, make your list, and get out and enjoy a pint or two along with good craic.

Chicago: Downtown

D4 Irish Pub & Café

345 East Ohio Street
312/624-8385
www.d4pub.com

Fans of Irish pubs flock to this new place located in Streeterville. Named for a Dublin zip code, this place has the look and feel of a modern Dublin pub. Great menu favorites served with Irish flair, and a variety of Irish whiskey and stout. You'll find a rare copy of The Book of Kells on display. This alone is worth the visit.

Dublin's Bar & Grill

1050 North State Street
312/266-6340

They open early for breakfast. Irish favorites are included on the menu along with delicious pub food. Enjoy the outdoor patio on warm summer nights.

The Kerryman

661 North Clark Street
312/335-8121
www.thekerrymanchicago.com

Here's where you'll meet up with the real Irish. One of the owners, Micheal O'Donoghue (correct spelling), plays for St. Brendan's Gaelic Football Club, so you're sure to hear talk of the game. Delicious food served in huge quantities, all-day Irish breakfast (the cook is from Limerick). Monday is Industry Night, which means a 25 percent discount on bar tabs. Their patio dining is not to be missed.

The Kerryman, Chicago - great food and good craic.

Lizzie McNeill's

400 North McClurg Court
312/467-1992

Good pub grub, TVs, jukebox and a great view of the river from the outdoor patio.

O'Brien's Riverwalk Café

On the Chicago River at Wabash and Wacker

312/346-3131

Seasonal—open only when the weather warms and summer breezes blow. Good food selection, terrific views of Chicago's architectural excellence as you wine and dine on Chicago's riverfront. Be prepared to rough it; port-a-potties are provided for customer use.

O'Leary's Public House

541 North Wells Street

312/661-1306

Offers a good selection of pub grub, TV's for viewing sportscasts, and outdoor seating in the summer.

O'Neil's

152 West Ontario Street

312/787-5269

Heated beer garden with picnic tables gives this place a cozy neighborhood feeling to be enjoyed year round. Catch live sports on the TVs scattered around the pub. Good pub grub, chocolate surprise with every order.

Poag Mahone's

333 South Wells Street

312/566-9100

www.poagmahones.com

You'll love the feel of this classic turn-of-the-century style bar. They serve up great traditional pub food and a good two-pour Guinness. Excellent place to grab a tasty lunch or early dinner.

Shamrock Club

210 West Kinzie Street

312/321-9314

River North's neighborhood bar. Lunchtime and happy-hour crowds are friendly and large in this narrow place. A sidewalk cafe seats a total of 16, so get there early to secure your view of Chicago.

Chicago: North Side

Casey Moran's

3660 North Clark Street

773/755-4444

www.kincadesbar.com

Good place to unwind after the game. This Wrigleyville neighborhood pub offers plenty of seating, comfortable heated patio with retractable roof for year-round dining, excellent pub fare. Sportscasts from all over the world are shown on 25 53-inch plasma TVs.

Corcoran's

1615 North Wells Street
312/440-0885

Comfortable outdoor cafe, good pub grub, TVs featuring live sportscasts, Irish music and rock, pub-crawls featured the first Tuesday of every month.

Emerald Isle

6686 North Northwest Highway
773/775-2848

Fun neighborhood pub featuring a great outdoor patio. Full menu includes appetizers with Southwestern and Irish fare. Live bands on the weekends, DJs on Thursday nights, flat-screen TVs for sporting events, darts, video bowling, and electronic trivia.

Emmit's Pub & Eatery

495 North Milwaukee Avenue
312/563-9631
www.emmits.com

You just might run into a Hollywood producer. Many films have been shot here, including *Ocean's 11*, *Ocean's 12*, *Backdraft*, *Uncle Buck*, *Only the Lonely*, and several others. The unusual decor includes traditional Irish items as well as official Chicago Police paraphernalia. Good food, good brew, and good craic.

Fifth Province Pub

4626 North Knox Avenue
773/282-7035
www.irishamhc.com

Located inside the Irish American Heritage Center, this cozy pub serves up good food along with an excellent selection of Irish beer and whiskey. Live Irish music. Open Friday and Saturday evenings. Free parking.

Galvin's Public House

5901 West Lawrence Avenue
773/205-0570

Traditional Irish breakfast served all day. Lunch and dinner items include Irish and American cuisine. Outdoor dining is available in the summer. View all the GAA, soccer, hurling, and rugby games on their many TVs. Two dart boards and bowling games.

John Barleycorn

659 West Belden Avenue
773/348-8899
www.johnbarleycorn.com

Choose good grub from their international menu plus Chicago-style cheesecake served in their lovely outdoor dining area. There's plenty of TVs for sports fans, plus a jukebox to get the place hopping.

Johnny O'Hagan's

3374 North Clark Street
773/248-3600
www.johnnyohagans.com

Extensive menu items including Irish fare, cozy atmosphere with lots of fine detail. Dine in their lovely outdoor eating area or inside, where you can view sportscasts on the many TVs scattered throughout.

Kelly's

949 West Webster Avenue
773/281-0656

Mucho TVs for watching sportscasts. Irish and college crowd frequent this pub. Good food served for lunch and dinner and a great outdoor beer garden for relaxing with your friends.

McNamara's

4328 West Irving Park Road
773/725-1800

Large dining room with outdoor seating. Traditional Irish menu served, along with good burgers. Brunch is served on Saturday and Sunday, and you'll find TVs for watching the games. Irish breakfast served on weekends.

Monsignor Murphy's

3019 North Broadway
773/348-7285
www.monsignormurphys.com

Cozy hole-in-the-wall pub located on the second floor of an old brownstone. Good pub grub served in the outdoor garden. Plenty of TVs, pool tables, dartboards and video games.

Murphy's Bleachers

3655 North Sheffield Avenue
773/281-5356
www.murphysbleachers.com

Enjoy great burgers across the street from Wrigley Field. Good selection of appetizers and sandwiches and pizza. TVs, video games and bean bag games outside in the outdoor cafe.

Mystic Celt

3443 North Southport Avenue
773/529-8550
www.mysticceltchicago.com

Traditional Irish pub combines with a comfortable lounge including candlelit booths. Irish and American food served along with their Sunday brunch. TVs available for viewing of sportscasts, DJ on weekends. Outdoor seating.

O'Brien's

1528 North Wells Street
312/787-3131
www.obriensrestaurant.com

Boasts the largest outdoor patio in the city. Serves steak and seafood. Live entertainment, TVs for local sportscasts.

O'Donovan's

2100 West Irving Park Road
773/478-2100
www.kincadesbar.com

Great family place and dog-friendly. Martinis and manicures are every first and third Tuesday of the month; magic shows performed every Friday, Saturday, and Sunday from 10 am to 3 pm. Their sidewalk cafe is open in the spring and summer. You'll love the great menu selections, including corn dog appetizers. Six high-definition big-screen TVs are scattered throughout the bar area where you can view American sports as well as European soccer matches.

Paddy Long's

1028 West Diversey Parkway

773/290-6988

Irish breakfast served all day, along with a full menu offering good cooking at reasonable prices. TVs are usually tuned to rugby and football while the locals chow down on fish and chips and hot wings. Good selection of beer. Stop in and say hello to one of the owners; they hail from Dublin.

Trinity Bar

2721 North Halsted Street

773/880-9293

Check out their $3 Guinness everyday special. This place has everything: three separate bars on three levels, a full kitchen, and twenty HD plasma TVs playing all the best games.

Chicago: South Side

Cork & Kerry

10614 South Western Avenue

773/445-2675

www.corkandkerrychicago.com

Enjoy beer, shots, and mixed drinks in the year-round beer garden. Free popcorn and the random free pizza during the World Series.

Dempsey's Irish American Grill

6520 South Cicero Avenue

708/594-5500

Located near Midway Airport, this delightful eatery serves up not only the finest Shepherd's pie and chicken cooked in Irish whiskey, but also your favorite Irish beers. If you're a fan of boxing, you'll enjoy their elevated dining area roped off to resemble a boxing ring. This serves as a tribute to the famous Irish-American boxer Jack Dempsey. You'll find his boxing gloves encased in glass by the entrance door, along with countless photos and newspaper clippings lining the walls. Parking available.

Gilhooley's Grande Saloon

3901 West 103rd Street

773/233-2200

www.gilhooleyssxu.com

Located adjacent to and owned by St. Xavier University, they serve daily lunch and dinner specials featuring homemade soda bread. Every other Wednesday features open mic night and karaoke on Thursday nights. Friday and Saturday nights they host live bands. Enjoy the ambiance of their outdoor patio.

Grace O'Malley's

1416 South Michigan Avenue
312/588-1800
www.graceomalleyschicago.com

Great place for good times and tasty Irish fare. Cozy up to the comfortable bar and seating area and enjoy good conversation. Join in the Sunday "morning after." They serve a full breakfast with a Bloody Mary to wash it down. Comes complete with blue cheese olives.

Hackney's

733 South Dearborn Street
312/461-1116
www.hackneysprintersrow.net

Full range of menu items mixed with lovely patio seating makes for a relaxing afternoon or evening in this Printer's Row neighborhood. Call for information on live entertainment.

McGann's Pub

11532 South Western Avenue
773/233-7700

A great place to unwind and watch the game. Enjoy the daily buffet served in the pub, including a huge salad bar, home-made soups, and delicious desserts.

Schaller's Pump

3714 South Halsted Street
773/376-6332

Bridgeport neighborhood family-owned bar and gathering place for Sox fans. Tasty pub grub with all your favorite Irish drinks. A great place to kick back and enjoy an evening of good craic with friends and neighbors.

Northwest Suburbs

Durty Nellie's

180 North Smith Street, Palatine
847/358-9150
www.durtynellies.com

This isn't a place to slip in for a short one, as this mega pub boasts multiple beer gardens, rooftop terrace for alfresco dining, and a mezzanine level overlooking the stage, featuring live music. Their menu includes a selection of unique and delicious entrees.

Finn McCool's

1941 East Algonquin Road, Schaumburg
847/303-5100
www.finnmccoolschicago.com

Enjoy full coverage of your favorite sporting events on 30 large flat-screen TVs, including one 50-inch screen. Tabletop speakers can be tuned to each individual table's game of choice to hear the play-by-play. Enjoy their outdoor patio area, extensive menu, and sports and trivia video games on the NTN satellite network using cordless "playmaker" units to compete with players in bars across North America. Visit their other location at 72 North Williams Street in Crystal Lake.

Irish Mill Inn

26592 Nort IL-83, Mundelein

847/566-7044

www.irishmillinn.com

This best-kept secret in the northwest suburbs features tasty pub grub at reasonable prices, friendly bartenders, and "raise the rafters" entertainment. Enjoy your selection of food and brew in their open air dining area.

Irish Mill Inn, Mundelein.

South and Southwest Suburbs

Ashford House Restaurant/Bar

7959 West 159th Street, Tinley Park

708/633-7600

Some of the best Irish cuisine in town. Irish breakfast served seven days a week, all day. Owned and operated by Winston's Irish Food Store located right next door.

Carraig Pub

Chicago Gaelic Park

6119 West 147th Street, Oak Forest

708/687-9323

www.chicagogaelicpark.org

This is where the Irish hang their caps. Authentic Irish pub located in the heart of Gaelic Park. Experience the ambiance of a real Irish pub. Enjoy the best Guinness on the South Side. The food is amazing and reasonably priced. You'll find great entertainment and good craic.

Jack Desmond's Irish Pub & Restaurant

10339 South Ridgeland Avenue, Chicago Ridge

708/857-7910

www.jackdesmonds.com

Authentic Irish Pub, Irish and American bands on weekends, karaoke competitions, drink specials every day, beer garden and great authentic Irish cuisine.

McCool's Irish Pub & Restaurant

1600 West 16th Street, Oakbrook

630/371-7880

Delicious and reasonably priced cuisine served in a relaxing atmosphere. The menu offers Irish selections along with traditional American fare.

Sam Maguire's

39 Orland Square Drive, Orland Park
708/460-1771
www.sammaguires.net

Always packed on weekends with patrons enjoying live music, beanbag toss competitions, and a cozy beer garden. Join in the Monday and Sunday evening karaoke and Wednesday's Texas Holdem League.

Murphy's Law

9247 South Cicero Avenue,
Oak Lawn
708/636-1555

You can always count on a crowd and good craic. This neighborhood pub serves food until 6 pm. After that, it's pizza. Good prices, full-service bar.

Murphy's Steakhouse and Pub

10160 West 191st Street, Mokena
708/479-6873
www.murphysofmokena.com

Great place to unwind and enjoy delicious food and monthly drink specials. Join in their bean bag bournament, Texas Holdem, karaoke, along with live entertainment. On Sunday and Tuesdays the kids eat free with each adult entree purchased. Visit their Web site for the events schedule.

Quigley's Irish Pub

4010 West 111th Street, Oak Lawn
708/952-4774

Lively suburban bar to enjoy bands and loud music. Call for entertainment schedule.

West Suburbs

Doc Ryan's

7432 West Madison Street,
Forest Park
708/366-2823
www.docryans.com

A comfortable beer garden and rooftop deck make this a great summer hang out. The second floor entertainment area offers darts and video games. Good variety of pub grub, featuring appetizers and pizza. Live music.

McGaffer's Saloon

7737 West Roosevelt Road,
Forest Park
708/366-9707

Delivers that old-style service and atmosphere. Enjoy their outstanding outdoor patio, traditional Irish pub grub, and your favorite sports games on the many TVs found throughout the pub. Video games to keep you occupied while enjoying a beer or two.

Quigley's

43 East Jefferson Street, Naperville
630/428-4774
www.quigleysirishpub.net

An authentic Irish pub, designed, built, and shipped over from Ireland. They offer an extensive menu of good pub grub with a few traditional Irish dishes. Enjoy a tender slab of Guinness Ribs on their outdoor patio. Irish breakfast served on weekends until 5 pm, live music Thursday through Saturday. Catch your favorite games on the many TVs scattered around the pub.

Shannon's

428 North Main Street, Glen Ellyn
630/790-9080

Enjoy their extensive menu offering traditional fare underneath their covered and heated outdoor patio. Watch your favorite teams on their many TVs. Good place to begin your weekend of fun.

Northwest Indiana

T.J. Maloney's Authentic Irish Pub

800 East 81st Avenue, Merrillville, Indiana
219/755-0569
www.tjmaloneys.com

We can't leave our Indiana neighbors out. This place is amazing for their reasonable three-course dinners, first-class entertainment, and outdoor patio—well worth the trip.

Just Good Craic and Occasional Music

Some folks prefer thirst-quenching brew, good conversation, and the company of others over assorted menu selections, outdoor patios, and musicians. In Ireland the pub is an extension of the home—the place to socialize. Cross an Irish threshold and you may be offered the traditional Céad Míle Fáilte (pronounced KAYD mee-luh-FAWL-cha, which is Irish for "one hundred thousand welcomes.") If you're looking for serious conversation and good company, check out some of the places listed below. Invite a companion and buy the first round.

Chicago: North Side

Cuneen's

1438 West Devon Avenue
773/555-1212

Great place for good conversation, laidback atmosphere. There's a pool table and a TV for sportscasts.

Foley's

1841 West Irving Park Road
773/929-1210

Cozy neighborhood pub, TV for sportscasts, darts and video games.

Galway Bay Pub

500 West Diversey Parkway

773/348-3750

Free popcorn comes with good conversation and lively socialization. This is truly the pub to visit for good craic, TV for sportscasts, darts, pool table, electronic trivia, and video games.

Gunther Murphy's

1638 West Belmont Avenue

773/472-5139

www.gunthermurphys.com

Stop in for entertainment scheduled each night. You'll find live music on weekends, open mic nights, comedy nights, and Bluegrass music. Join in a game of darts, golden tee, or electronic trivia.

Halligan Bar

2274 North Lincoln Avenue

773/472-7940

www.halliganbarchicago.com

Every night they feature a special on drinks. Watch games on TV and get involved in their competitive Golden Tee.

Irish Eyes

2519 North Lincoln Avenue

773/348-9548

Catch the live music on Friday and Saturday nights, along with a game of darts or Golden Tee.

Mulligan's Public House

2000 West Roscoe Street

773/549-4225

www.mulliganspublichouse.com

You'll find some serious dart players here. After the matches, turn to the TVs for the sportscasts.

Poitin Stil

1502 West Jarvis Street

773/338-3285

Galway folks will feel right at home in this pub with accent colors of maroon and gold. Live music on Friday and Saturday, open mic on Thursdays.

River Shannon

425 West Armitage Avenue

312/944-5087

This place has been around for over 60 years. Lively place filled with antiques. Sit yourself down, order a pint, watch sports on big screen TVs, and enjoy good conversation.

Six Penny Bit

5800 West Montrose Avenue

773/545-2033

Where the Irish go to watch the Gaelic football games on the large TV. You can enjoy a game of darts or pool while enjoying the ambiance of a true Irish bar.

Vaughan's Pub

2917 North Sheffield Avenue
773/281-8188

Open mic on Tuesdays, DJs Thursdays through Saturday, plenty of TVs for the sports fans, and it's okay to bring the dog—pet-friendly place.

Chicago: South Side

Dugan's

128 South Halsted Street
312/421-7191
www.dugansonhalsted.com

Live music on weekends, hockey, foosball, darts, jukebox, video bowling and beanbag games. They have menus from neighboring restaurants; have food delivered.

Hinky Dink's

3243 West 111st Street
773/445-1598

Unique spot to join in with locals for good craic and brew. If you're interested in how the pub got its name, seek out the owner; he'll be sure to fill your ear with interesting stories.

Keegan's Pub

10618 South Western Avenue
773/233-6829

Live music on weekends, TVs for sportscast viewing, jukebox.

MacKell's Inn

3259 West 111th Street
773/445-9181

Bands on Sunday, open mic on Thursday, TVs, jukebox and Gold Tee Golf will keep you entertained. Good neighborhood place to sit and relax.

McDuffy's

11050 South Spaulding Avenue
773/779-3033

Irish dance club, popular among young South Side Irish.

McNallys

11136 South Western Avenue
773/779-6202

TVs, darts, and video games will keep you entertained. Good place to find loyal White Sox fans.

Mitchell's Tap

3356 South Halsted Street
773/927-6073

Although not your typical Irish pub, this Bridgeport tavern stocks 35 varieties of beer, including Guinness, Harp, Killean Red and more. This cozy neighborhood place offers bowling and golf machines, as well as darts. Parking is available.

Mrs. O'Leary's Dubliner

10910 South Western Avenue

773/238-0784

Darts and TV are featured along with authentic Irish ambiance. Stop in for some good conversation.

Schinnick's

3758 South Union Avenue

773/523-8591

Bridgeport's oldest Irish pub. Established in 1938, it has been in the Schinnick family for three generations. If you're a serious White Sox fan, you'll love this place. There's no kitchen but there are plenty of TVs for watching the games.

Sullivan's Kolmar Liquors

4535 West Marquette Road

773/767-3281

This South Side Irish pub is frequented by many firefighters. This neighborhood place will feel like home in no time at all, for the friendly bartenders cater to all customers.

T.R.'s Pub

3908 West 111th Street

773/239-4554

Good place to unwind and watch the games on their large screen TVs.

West Suburbs

Duffy's Tavern

7513 West Madison Street, Forest Park

708/366-3887

Here is where you can get involved in everything sports. They sponsor volleyball leagues and invite everyone to watch the international games on their TVs. Partake in dart games, electronic bowling and Golden Tee. Good neighborhood place to meet up and join in.

James Joyce Irish Pub

7138 Windsor Avenue, Berwyn

708/795-1100

www.thejamesjoyceirishpub.com

Owned by two fellows from Ireland. You'll be welcomed into this cozy pub. Join in their quiz nights every Tuesday. TVs are available for watching the Gaelic games. Find good conversation in this friendly neighborhood bar.

Murphy's Pub

7414 West Madison Street, Forest Park

708/366-3008

DJs on Wednesdays and Fridays, karaoke on Thursdays, lots of TVs, dartboards and Golden Tee Golf to entertain. Put this traditional Irish bar on your must visit list.

Fitzgerald's

6615 West Roosevelt Road, Berwyn
708/788-2118

A great spot for live entertainment featuring blues, rock, and jazz. Famous for their outdoor music festivals hosted under huge tents. You'll enjoy the charming ambiance of this place, which was built in 1920, but resembles the classic bars of the 1940s.

Healy's Westside

7321 West Madison Street,
Forest Park
708/366-4277

Good neighborhood place to unwind with a pint and a few mini corndogs for a soakage. Notice the floor when you walk in because it's over 100 years old. There are lots of classic details to this place. Occasionally you'll hear a live band, there are lots of TVs scattered throughout and dart boards.

McNally's Traditional Irish Pub

201 East Main Street, St. Charles
630/513-6300

Live bands on weekends and you can watch your favorite sporting events on their large screen TVs. Cozy up to the inviting fireplace and check out their fine beer and whiskey selections.

Southwest Suburbs

An Seanachi

2825 West Burr Oak Avenue,
Blue Island
708/385-6744

You might just hear some good stories coming from the locals. Cozy up to this friendly bar, enjoy karaoke and DJ on Tuesdays, and play the jukebox.

The Goal Post Irish American Pub

5207 West 95th Street, Oak Lawn
708/422-5275

Good pub to view all sporting events, and the bartenders will gladly pour a pint or two.

March and St. Patrick's Day

Chicago's Downtown Irish Parade.
(Courtesy of Dean Battaglia.)

The world's first St. Patrick's Day parade occurred on March 17, 1762, in New York City and featured Irish soldiers serving in the English military. As Irish immigrants moved out across the United States, St. Patrick's Day celebrations went with them. Chicago held its first parade in 1843, a proud moment for the many Irish whose ancestors had to fight stereotypes and prejudice to find acceptance in America. In 1956 Mayor Richard J. Daley moved Chicago's St. Patrick's Day Parade downtown for the first time since 1916, where it became the city's biggest annual political event. In 1995 Congress proclaimed March as Irish American Heritage Month, and each year the president of the United States issues an Irish American Month proclamation.

Irish is the nation's second most frequently reported ancestry. Chicago's Cook County boasts of being home to over 500,000 who claim to be Irish descendants. That's a lot of corned beef and cabbage, not to mention the parades. And we're not just talking about your ordinary, everyday parade. The pageantry, grandeur, and magnitude of this Chicago event is unprecedented anywhere else in the world. Unmistakable for the whine of bagpipes, the sassy Irish dancers, the mischievous leprechauns, and the beautifully decorated floats, Chicago's Irish know how to host St. Patrick's Day.

So you'll not miss out on any of the festivities, I've included parade locations around the city and suburbs. Although you're sure to miss a few, the good news is you'll have at least three weekends to participate because the parades are scheduled a week or two before March 17th. So in the old tradition, pin shamrocks on your lapel, take your place on the parade route, and join the thousands of Irish Americans who celebrate their heritage, Chicago-style.

Cardinal Francis George, The Honorable Mayor Daley, Senator Dick Durbin, Esteemed General Chairman and Honored Guest. (Courtesy of Dean Battaglia.)

St. Patrick's Day Parades: Take in a Parade or Two or Three!

Chicago's Downtown Parade

312/942-9188
www.chicagostpatsparade.com

The Parade begins at noon and runs on Columbus from Balboa to Monroe. Thousands line up along Columbus Drive the Saturday before St. Patrick's Day (unless St. Patrick's Day falls on a Saturday). This Chicago tradition features over 30 bands, 50 floats, and thousands of marchers and leprechauns. The winner of the St. Patrick's Day Queen Contest leads the parade in a horse-drawn carriage. Witness the Chicago River changing from its usual murkiness to the emerald-green color reminiscent of Ireland; festivities start with the dyeing of the Chicago River, a tradition since 1962. Try to get a spot by the rail east of Michigan Avenue; the Dye Boat does not go west of that bridge. The dye process

The Chicago River goes green in honor of St. Patrick's Day. (Courtesy of Dean Battaglia.)

usually takes place between 10:15 am and 11:00 am. Your best bet is to take public transportation because parking lots fill up quickly and are expensive. Exit at any of the Blue or Red Line stops in the Loop and walk east a few blocks to Columbus. If you do decide to drive, try the underground Grand Park garage, the Hilton at Balboa and Michigan, or other nearby lots.

South Side Parade

773/393-8687
www.southsideirishparade.org

Held the Sunday before St. Paddy's Day, the parade route is from 103rd and Western to 115th and Western. Originally called the Southtown Parade, it was moved downtown in 1960. A 13-block stretch is home to a proud tradition that weaves family fun with boisterous revelry. The parade day begins with Irish songs and music at 8:30 am, followed by Mass at 9 am at St. Cajetan Church (112th & Artesian, in the west Morgan Park neighborhood of Chicago). Folks begin to line the parade route on South Western Avenue as early as 10 am. (The east side of Western is dry. All bars are located on the west side. That makes the east side more family oriented, the West side better for hearty partiers). Approximately 120 families, schools, civic organizations, and businesses march along the parade route through the Beverly and Morgan Park neighborhoods. But the party doesn't end there. Take a gander at the following three activities to see what's going on before, during, and after the parade in that South Side neighborhood.

Beverly Arts Center

2407 West 111th Street

773/445-3838

Family Fest starts at noon. You can watch the parade from inside the center. Live music and movies for children. Food and beverages will be served. Bands begin at 8 pm after a performance by the Pipes and Drums of Emerald Society.

Sam Maguire's Irish Pub and Restaurant

39 Orland Square Drive, Orland Park

708/460-1771

"Kegs & Eggs" breakfast, 8 am, Sunday, includes round-trip bus ride for the South Side Irish parade. Fee includes beer on the bus. Leprechauns, Irish dancers, and bagpipers provide entertainment well into the evening.

Gaelic Park

6119 West 147th Street, Oak Forest

708/687-9323

www.chicagogaelicpark.org

Celebrate Ireland on Parade, a festival of music and dance with local musicians and dance schools. Join in one of the South Side's longest-standing traditions with a celebration of Mass at 9 am followed by an authentic Irish breakfast. Immediately after breakfast, round-trip transportation is provided to the South Side Parade for all those who wish to march with Gaelic Park. After the parade the entire facility comes to life with activity. A delicious hot-food buffet is served.

Naperville

630/375-7725

www.wsirish.org

Celebrate your Irish heritage and join the west suburban Irish for their annual St. Patrick's Day Parade. The parade kicks off at 10 am from Naperville North High School, located at 899 North Mill Street. The parade continues south on Mill Street, east on Jefferson Avenue, south on Main Street, and west on Jackson Avenue to Centennial Beach. This is a good sized parade. Represented are local politicians, businesses, families, charitable organizations, etc. The whole town turns out for this colorful event with green hats, beads, and T-shirts. Check their Web site for the dates and for other Irish events sponsored by this organization.

West Suburban Irish Parade, Naperville.

Northwest Side Irish Parade

www.northwestsideirish.org

This organization is relatively new, founded in 2003. Their St. Patrick's Day parade kicks off at noon on the first Sunday in March (check their Web site to be sure for dates and times). Beginning at Onahan School at 6333 West Raven, the parade route is Raven south on Neola west onto Northwest Highway to Harlem. The review stand is located at Northwest Highway and Raven Street. It features live entertainment, including bagpipes, and you might just see the kids from the North Side Youth Gaelic Football Club decked out in green. Don't miss the after-parade party held at the VFW hall, 10 West Higgins Road (Higgins at Canfield) in Park Ridge. The price of admission includes live entertainment, food, and beverages (alcoholic and nonalcoholic). Usher in the month of St. Paddy's celebrations by attending this lively celebration. Visit their Web site for additional information.

Forest Park Irish Parade

www.forestparkchamberofcommerce.org

Usually held the first Saturday in March, this increasingly popular parade is anything but small town. Kicking off at 1 pm, the 80-plus entries march their way down Van Buren and Madison and travel east on Madison to Elgin. Spend the day shopping the unique and charming collection of boutiques and galleries as you visit each restaurant and tavern for Irish fare specials. Visit the chamber's Web site for any change in dates and times.

St. Charles Irish Parade

630/584-8384
www.dtown.org/events/st_patrick.asp

This parade boasts Leprechaun stilt walkers, an Irish Queen, and a whole lot of Irish shenanigans and is sponsored by the St. Charles Chamber of Commerce. Check their Web site for date and time.

Elmhurst St. Patrick's Day Parade

630/834-0300
www.elmhurststpatsparade.com

Join this community in celebration. Usually set for the Saturday before St. Patrick's Day, it steps off at Wilson Street and Spring Road. It's a small local parade, but you'll find beautifully decorated floats, bagpipers, and fun and entertainment. If you'd like to avoid the large crowds, this parade is for you. Visit their Web site for any change in information.

Lake Villa Irish Parade

Lake Villa
847/356-6100
www.lake-villa.org

Bagpipe marching bands, Irish dancers, beauty queens, politicians, Boy and Girl Scouts, and fire trucks all lead the march south on McKinley Avenue. Visit their Web site for information on the scheduled date and time.

Tinley Park Irish Parade

Oak Park Avenue Main Street Association

17036 South Oak Park Avenue, Tinley Park

708/532-9989
www.opama.org

This parade is usually held the first Saturday in March. You'll find professionally decorated floats, along with amateur floats and walking groups. Organizations such as Gaelic Park and the South Side Irish enter floats in competition. If the weather cooperates, you can sip hot chocolate or Irish coffee while sitting at one of the many cafes along the parade route. Visit their Web site for details.

Durbin's Restaurant and Pub

17265 Oak Park Avenue, Tinley Park
708/429-1000
www.durbinspub.com

You've no doubt worked up an appetite for good pub grub and Irish brew. So head to Durbin's where you'll spend the day enjoying Irish dancers, bagpipers, music, and a variety of activities for the wee little ones. Green beer flows and traditional corned beef and cabbage specials crowd the menu. And don't miss the activity in this place the Saturday night before St. Paddy's Day; it's guaranteed to fit your definition of a grand celebration. Durbin's arranges bus transportation to the South Side Irish Parade. Visit their Web site for details.

March Events: Wearin' o' the Green

St. Patrick's Day is one of the most recognized national holidays on the global calendar and offers the excuse to party from Brookfield to Brussels, Moscow to Moline. Even reclusive North Korea sends annual greetings to Irish President MacAlese, and Shanghai most recently held its first official St. Patrick's Day party. March 17 is the one day of the year when everyone is a wee bit Irish. (Whether folks know it or not, they are commemorating the death of Maewyn Succat, also known as Patrick, the patron saint of Ireland. St. Patrick was credited with bringing Christianity to Ireland in the fifth century A.D.)

Chicago celebrates its Irish in grand style. It dyes the river green, and each of the suburbs responds with a flourish of Guinness kegs. Shop windows display paper shamrocks, green plastic hats, and Irish flags. Eager onlookers line parade routes, while children sit still long enough to have their faces painted with the colors of Ireland. Chicago's Sears Tower and Hancock Building light up green after sundown.

Sure it's the parties, the green beer, the emerald-colored lights, and the corned beef and cabbage, but there's more. There's a history to this celebration—an importance—a reason why the Irish insist on wearing the green and celebrating way into the night.

The Irish immigrants came to America to escape the hunger and distressing poverty of Ireland, putting great distance between themselves and England; wearin' of the green meant certain death for those brave souls intent on preserving the Irish custom and heritage in Ireland.

Once in America, the Irish filled the streets with green on March 17 to show their numbers and their unity. Even General George Washington honored the great faith of St. Patrick by giving Irish troops under his command a holiday on March 17, 1780. And to this day, Irish Americans gather and fill the air with sounds of pipes and drums—proud to be Irish and proud to be Americans.

Chicago and its suburbs roll out the green carpet—there's something for everyone. Be sure to get plenty of rest before St. Paddy's Day; you'll be busy from early morning well into the next day (and the next if you plan it right). Your biggest dilemma will be how to get all the events squeezed into such a short amount of time.

And don't forget to wear your green. According to the legend of the leprechaun, if you're not wearin' the green you'll surely be pinched by the mischievous wee Irish sprout himself. (To set the record straight, the terms "Emerald Isle" and "the wearing of the shamrock" have popularized the notion that green is the official color of Ireland when, in fact, the official color is blue.)

Be sure and check with your neighborhood churches, park districts, and pubs for information on their St. Patrick's Day celebrations, because, as sure as it rains in Ireland, you can bet that every Irish pub in this city will host the perfect party. Check out the charitable events; not only do the Irish celebrate in grand style but they also value the opportunity to contribute to worthy causes.

Note: The following St. Patrick's Day events are scheduled before or on March 17. Visit the Web sites or call for dates, times, and locations.

Chicago

Boat Cruises

St. Patrick's Day Cruise

600 East Grand Avenue
877/299-7854
www.mysticbluecruises.com

Mystic Blue Cruises offer lunch and dinner cruises, featuring a variety of Irish-themed cuisine, music, dancing, entertainment, festive decorations, and favors, along with incredible views of the world famous Chicago skyline. Call for reservations.

St. Patrick's Day History Cruise

Illinois Street and Streeter Drive
312/222-9328
www.shorelinesightseeing.com

Glide down the Chicago River and learn about the role the Irish played in shaping Chicago in this themed cruise from Shoreline Sightseeing. Includes buffet, soft drinks, Irish music, and cash bar. Tickets available online, by phone, or at the dock, if space is available.

Charity Benefits

Bank of America "Shamrock Shuffle"

312/904-9814
www.shamrockshuffle.com

The runners meet at Grant Park for the world's largest 8K race. It features runners, a 5K walk, and a Kids Quarter-Mile Shuffle. More than 80 charities benefit from this run/walk. Visit their Web site for date and time.

Bank of America's (LaSalle Bank) Shamrock Shuffle. (Courtesy of Bank of America/LaSalle Bank.)

Chiditarod, Chicago Urban Shopping Cart Race

www.chiditarod.org.

A charity shopping cart race to collect for food pantries throughout the city. Teams are encouraged to decorate their carts and themselves (you must supply your own cart). Wrap your carts in shamrocks, green tinsel, and funny hats. Drape yourself in green feather boas and go nuts! Prizes will be rewarded for the most creative teams. Contenders should have 15 pounds of food at the finish line. Cart qualifications? Anything goes, but no motors or pedal assistance. Usually held the first Saturday in March. Call to reserve a spot.

The Clerys, Forakers, and Phil Bossard join in the Chiditarod.

Friends of Alcott School St. Paddy's Day 5K Run/Walk and Kids' Leprechaun Leap at Diversey Harbor

773/868-3010
www.chicagoevents.com

Be green and be seen this St. Patrick's Day. Bring your Irish spirit and your family out for this annual 5K Run/Walk, plus the Leprechaun Leap (kids' dashes). The race features long-sleeved T-shirts, a lakefront course, awards, and an indoor post-race party at Trinity Bar and Grill. Strollers and leashed dogs also welcome to join after the elite runners have begun. Preregister online. Check their Web site for date and time.

Mercy Home "Shamrocks for Kids"

312/738-4389
www.mercyhome.org

Volunteers hit the streets to hand out shamrock pins for a donation to this worthy cause. Affiliated with the Archdiocese of Chicago, Mercy Home is privately funded. Mercy provides a home for children who need a safe place to live. Get your organization, work place and neighborhood groups involved in this annual fundraiser. Individual volunteers are welcome as well. If you're interested in distributing the pins, call the number listed.

Young Irish Fellowship Club's Forever Green Bash

312/902-1943

www.youngirish.com

There's no better way to celebrate St. Patrick's Day than at Chicago's biggest and best St. Patrick's Day Bash—Forever Green. Held annually at Navy Pier's Grand Ballroom, there are over 2,000 celebrants who gather to enjoy the bands, bag pipers and Irish dancers. Food is available on a cash basis. Must be 21 or older to attend. Proceeds benefit various charitable organizations throughout the city. Post-event shuttle buses and trolleys are scheduled to provide transportation to and from this Navy Pier event. Visit their Web site for information on sponsored happy hours, sporting events (group tickets to the Cubs game), boat cruise on Lake Michigan, golf outing, trip to Ireland in November, and many other events. Their members also volunteer at a few of the Irish festivals throughout the city and attend cultural events as well.

Church Events

St. Barnabas Church's Mass and Soda Bread Reception

10134 South Longwood Drive

773/779-1166

www.stbarnabasparish.org

St. Patrick's Mass followed by a soda bread reception and a raffle for trips to Ireland.

St. Cajetan Church's Mass and Party

112th Street and Artestian Avenue

773/238-4100

Scheduled the morning of the South Side Irish Parade is an 8:30 am program of Irish songs and music, followed by a 9 am Mass. Don't miss their Official Pre-Parade Party (the night before the parade) at 8 pm in their Memorial Hall for entertainment, beer, wine, and snacks.

Cardinal Francis George, Honorable Mayor and Mrs. Daley celebrate St. Patrick's Day in style. (Courtesy of Dean Battaglia.)

Nativity of Our Lord Parish's Annual Party

653 West 37th Street

773/927-4479

www.nativitybridgeport.org

Usually held the Saturday before St. Patrick's Day, this annual party shouldn't be missed. A traditional Harrington's corned beef dinner, bagpipers, Irish dancers, disc jockey, and a night of dancing. Join in the raffle to win valuable prizes. Call for reservations.

Old St. Pat's Church's Siamsa Na Ngael

700 West Adams Street
312/648-1021
www.oldstpats.org

Join in their Siamsa Na Ngael honoring the feast of St. Patrick with unique, world-class Celtic entertainment. Special guest narrators have included many famous Hollywood names as well as a Pulitzer Prize winner. This elegant celebration is co-chaired by Mayor and Mrs. Daley and generates funding to support operational and capital costs of Old St. Pat's. Visit their Web site or call for dates and times.

St. Patrick's Day Civic Celebration

Join the Cardinal as he celebrates Mass at Old St. Pat's. Performances follow with Irish dancers, music, breakfast buffet and church tours.

Delectable Delights

Bobtail Soda Fountain's Guinness Ice Cream

2951 North Broadway Street
773/880-7372

3425 North Southport Avenue
773/248-6104

338 West Armitage Avenue
773/248-1439

1114 Central Avenue, Wilmette
847/251-0174

Also visit their location at Buckingham Fountain in Grant Park.

Five locations for you to sample their Guinness Ice Cream—sounds too good to be true! Even though they've cooked out the alcohol, you'll taste the malt through the cream, so don't worry about falling off the wagon with this scrumptious treat. Take some home, add a little Guinness, and treat yourself to a float. For those who prefer to stay away from the pub scene, this is one way to join in the celebration with a taste of stout.

Eli's Cheesecake's "Shake Your Shamrock"

6701 West Forest Preserve Avenue
773/205-3800
www.elischeesecake.com

"Shake Your Shamrock" festivities include Irish dancers and Irish music. Check out the bakery cafe for their St. Paddy's Day specials on delicious Irish Mint Cheesecake, only available during the month of March. Don't leave without sampling the Bailey's Cheesecake—not to be believed!

Misericordia Home's "Luck of the Irish" Sweets

6300 North Ridge Avenue
773/973-6300
www.misericordia.com

Celebrate St. Paddy's Day with a gift of sweets. Misericordia's gift-of-the-month club for March features delectable Irish goodies made with love by bakers-in-residence. Order their "Luck of the Irish" basket of soda bread, shamrock brownies, and other assorted chocolate goodies for family and friends. Contact them for details.

Entertainment

Beverly Arts Center's Irish Film Festival and Green Bagels

2407 West 111th Street

773/445-3838

www.beverlyartcenter.org

Don't miss their Irish Film Festival, usually scheduled for the first week in March. (Detailed information in Theater Chapter.) The BAC is the perfect place to view the South Side Irish Parade. Secure a seat indoors by the window. Live music, movies, and fun cultural activities planned for the day. A great place to take the kids and relax with your friends before heading out to the pubs.

Don't forget to order your bagels. Green bagels and cream cheese have become a traditional family breakfast on the morning of the South Side St. Patrick's Day Parade, thanks to the BAC Auxiliary Board. You can order online or at the BAC.

Irish Market and Beverly Rose of Tralee

11172 South Artesian Avenue

773/239-3927

www.chicagoroseoftralee.com,
www.bapa.org

Chicago's Beverly Area Planning Association sponsors an Irish Market to promote Chicago's Rose of Tralee. Usually held the first Saturday in March, this event takes place in the shops located between Wood Street and Longwood Drive. Numerous family activities will be offered throughout the day. Visit their Web site for details.

March Mayhem Boxing Event

Cicero Stadium

1909 South Laramie Avenue

312/226-5800

www.8countproductions.com

Visit their Web site to see what's on for March. They usually host an annual St. Patrick's Day professional boxing event offering world-class boxing.

Chicago Hauntings

610 North Clark Street

888/446-7891

www.chicagohauntings.com

Chicago's home-grown haunted tours company owned by *Chicago Haunts* author, Ursula Bielski, features a couple seasonal ghost tours:

Chief O'Neill Memorial Pub Crawl

Visit the Chief's haunted pub, learn the history of Bridgeport, meet the ghost of Harry Caray and toast the memory of Irish mob king Bugs Moran at the site of the St. Valentine's Day Massacre while hoisting a pint or two along the way. Besides a fully narrated tour, there will be door prizes and transportation via the ghost bus. Visit their Web site for dates and times. Book early; this tour fills up quickly.

Erin Go Boo

Chicago's Irish Ghost Tour. Travel along fabled Archer Avenue, visit the site of Engine 107, learn the curious past of Bishop Muldoon and creep through the storied enclave of Beverly's Irish Castle. Round off the evening with a drink to

Irish mob boss Bugs Moran at his favorite tavern. Irish coffee is included. Visit their Web site for dates and times. Book early.

Chicago Cultural Center's Threads of Ireland Tour

77 East Randolph Street
312/742-1190
www.chicagoneighborhoodtours.com

Join author Tom O'Gorman for an enlightening exploration of Chicago's Irish immigration history, legends, and more. Stop at Holy Name Cathedral and, later, visit Holy Family Church, located in Chicago's Near West Side community, when it's available. Tour the Irish American Heritage Center, and enjoy a drive through the historically Irish Bridgeport neighborhood to learn why and how Irish immigrants settled in the area. Fee includes lunch. Scheduled for only one day in March, so call for reservations.

Chicago History Museum Erin Go Beer! Irish Pubs of Chicago Trolley Tour

1600 North Clark Street
312/642-4600
www.chicagohs.org

Explore your inner leprechaun by visiting various historic pubs of Chicago via a private trolley. Learn about Irish immigration, Irish contributions to Chicago, folklore, history, and much more. Pubs visited on this trolley tour will be Celtic Crossings, Butch McGuire's, the Irish Oak, the Grafton, and the Abbey Pub.

North Park Village Nature Center's Children's St. Patrick's Day Events

5801 North Pulaski Road
312/744-5472
www.chicagoparkdistrict.com

Located on the northwest side of Chicago. Includes a 46-acre nature preserve and an educational facility that hosts children's St. Patrick's Day events. Call for schedule. Visit Chicago Park District Web site for information on all park district events.

Mt. Greenwood Library Children's Bingo

Chicago Public Library
11010 South Kedzie Avenue
312/747-2805
www.chipublib.org

St. Patrick's Day Bingo for Children.

Walker Library Storytelling and More

Chicago Public Library
11071 S. Hoyne Avenue
312/747-1920
www.chipublib.org

Story crafts, and performances. Call for details.

Irish Dancers Under the Picasso

City of Chicago
Daley Civic Center
www.cityofchicago.org

Dyeing of the Chicago River

Chicago River at Michigan Ave.

Starts at 10:45 am. Don't miss this big event before the parade on St. Patrick's Day.

House of Blues Irish Artists

329 North Dearborn Street
312/923-4408
www.hob.com

Check their Web site for an Irish performance during the week of March 17.

Irish American Heritage Center's St. Patrick's Day

4626 North Knox Avenue
773/282-7035
www.irishamhc.com

Festivities begin in early afternoon and go until midnight. You'll be treated to traditional and contemporary Irish music, dance, food, and kids' activities—a grand Hooley. Call to purchase tickets.

Pub and Restaurant Events

The pub is considered an extension of the home and supports a wide range of activities such as eating, drinking, and dancing. It is a resource shared by all, children included, and is a forum for discussions on every imaginable subject, from the earnest to the frivolous.

And let's not forget the food; if you've never before indulged in a full Irish breakfast, loosen your belt because this is truly a belly buster. You'll be served a variety of cereals, juices, and assorted breads for a meal that includes brown bread, scones, eggs, sausage (bangers), potatoes, grilled tomatoes, bacon (rashers), baked beans, black and white pudding, tea, and coffee. If you're a bit squeamish about certain foods, then you'd better ask about the pudding; it's not the dessert kind. You can't beat the pubs for delicious grub, and this is the week to get your fill of not only the Irish breakfast but potatoes and cabbage as well.

Here's a short list of pubs to get you started, but any pub you visit will surely be hosting a grand celebration.

North Side:

Abbey Pub

3420 West Grace Street
773/478-4408
www.abbeypub.com

Buses leave at 9 am. for the downtown parade. Football and hurling games telecast, Irish dancers, live music, and traditional food and drink available.

Atlantic Bar and Grill

5062 North Lincoln Avenue

773/506-7090

www.atlanticbar.homestead.com

Irish breakfast at 9 am. Followed by bagpipers, Irish dancers, and lives music. This charming Irish American tavern caters to urbanites and pint-drinking skippers alike.

Chief O'Neill's

3471 North Elston Avenue

773/583-3066

www.chiefoneillspub.com

Live music featuring Chief O'Neill's house band, Irish dancers, and delicious food served in a comfortable and spacious heated tent set up in their huge garden area. Don't miss out on their St. Paddy's Day Pig Roast. Featuring performances by musicians direct from Ireland. Enjoy their traditional Irish music sessions every Sunday night. The owners, All-Ireland Championship musicians, Brendan and Siobhan McKinney, invite you to enjoy great food and proper pints, the loveliest airs and reels, and all the other good craic at their fine establishment.

Emerald Loop Bar & Grill

216 North Wabash Avenue

312/263-0200

www.emeraldloopchicago.com

Opens early for a full Irish breakfast. DJ spins Irish tunes. Irish dancers, bagpipers, and green beer.

Fado

100 West Grand Avenue

312/836-0066

www.fadoirishpub.com

St. Baldrick's Day Fund Raiser. Managers and customers get their heads shaved to raise money for children with cancer. Enjoy the Irish dancers and live music. Visit their Web site or call for details on scheduled events.

Geja's Cafe

340 West Armitage Avenue

773/281-9101

www.gejascafe.com

Enjoy green cheese fondue with apples, grapes, and bread for dipping. Guinness and Baileys available to toast the celebration.

Harry Caray's

33 West Kinzie Street

312/828-0900

www.harrycarays.com

Live band, bagpipers perform, sandwiches and Irish specialties throughout the day.

Irish Eyes

2519 North Lincoln Avenue

773/348-9548

Pre-parade party. Have a few pints to warm you up before hopping on the CTA downtown for the parade. Live music and food.

Johnny O'Hagan's

3374 North Clark Street
773/248-3600
www.johnnyohagans.com

Six-nation rugby games on multiple screens at 8 am, followed by live music and a DJ.

McCormick & Schmick's

1 East Wacker Drive
312/923-7226
www.msmg.com

In past years they've hosted beer tastings. Great opportunity to have just a sip of your favorite Irish brews if you're not feeling up to a pint. Call for details on special events.

McFadden's

1206 North State Parkway
312/475-9450
www.mcfaddenschicago.com

Entertainment, bagpipers, stilt walkers, and Irish breakfast.

Mrs. Murphy and Sons Irish Bistro

3905 North Lincoln Avenue
773/248-3905
www.irishbisstro.com

The place to go for upscale dining while you enjoy Irish dancers, pipers, raffles, traditional corned beef and cabbage, and all the traditional Irish cuisine. Look for their in-house specials, which include:

boxty topped with smoked salmon and corned beef, glazed with hot brown sugar, topped with sour red cabbage and Dubliner cheese. Guinness rules and here; you'll find it in the onion soup, with white cheddar cheese oozing on top. Rooms available for private parties.

The Kerryman

661 North Clark Street
312/335-8121
www.thekerrymanchicago.com

Traditional Irish food, green beer, bagpipers, face painting, balloon artists. Irish breakfast, live sports telecasts from Ireland and all Notre Dame games shown on large screens.

South Side:

Corrigan's Pub

3047 West 111th Street
773/298-1315

You've stood watching the parade, waved your Irish flag, and cheered the numerous shamrock-laden floats. Now it's time to make your way to this fine establishment for some good Irish fun, including entertainment and tasty pub grub.

Cullinan's Stadium Club

11610 South Western Avenue
773/445-5620

Well-priced Guinness and Harp accompany the good food, American brew, and great fun. Enjoy an evening of music and good craic.

Fox's Beverly

9956 South Western Avenue

773/239-3212

Fox's Pub Orland Park,

9655 West 143rd Street, Orland Park

www.foxorland.com

Fox's Oak Lawn

**9240 South Cicero Avenue,
Oak Lawn**

708/499-2233

Three locations to serve up some fun the entire month of March during their "March Madness." This kid-friendly place provides Irish dancers, bagpipers, musicians, face painters, balloonists, and all the corned beef and cabbage you crave, plus other tasty menu items including their famous pizza. The food is fresh, homemade, and guaranteed to be right from the oven under the watchful eye of owner, Mary Theresa Scanlon Fox. You can even get your kids a ride on their South Side Irish Parade float. Fox's knows how to dish out a good time, and nobody does it better.

Kitty O'Shea's

720 South Michigan Avenue

312/294-6860

Located in the Hilton Hotel, they host a fine St. Patrick's Day Hooley with live music, good food, and traditional drink. Call for details.

Sean's Rhino Bar & Grill

10330 South Western Avenue

773/238-2060

Plenty of room in this tavern to throw back the much-touted Irish car bomb, should you find yourself in need of a rush of Guinness, Jameson and Bailey. You'll also find great grub, including pub pizza.

Suburbs

North and Northwest Suburbs

Delectable Delights

Capannari Ice Cream Shop's Seasonal Flavors

10 South Pine Street, Mt. Prospect

847/392-2277

www.capannaris.com

Don't let the name fool you; you'll find an Irishwoman behind the counter scooping some delectable treats. The taste of Ireland gets sweet for St. Paddy's Day, and this place celebrates in grand style by kicking off the ice cream season with a bit of Irish cheer. Stop in for their special flavors of Guinness, Irish Cream and Irish coffee in honor of the patron saint of Ireland. Visit their Web site for details.

Michael McPartlin scoops Guinness.
(Courtesy of Capannari's.)

Entertainment

Chicago Shamrox Lacrosse

5401 Trillium Boulevard, Suite 320, Hoffman Estates
877/SHAMROX
www.chicagoshamrox.com

Get set for a green celebration that is sure to please. Green jerseys, Irish dancers, bagpipers—plus you get to enjoy an action-packed game. Visit their Web site for details.

Metropolis Performing Arts Center's *Flanagan's Wake*

111 West Campbell Street, Arlington Heights
847/577-2121
www.metropolisarts.com

Reserve your seats for the production of *Flanagan's Wake*. Join the fictional villagers of Grapplin, County Sligo, as they tell tales, sing songs, and mourn the passing of one of their own. Check their Web site for details on dates and times.

Raue Center for the Arts St. Patrick's Day Production

26 North Williams Street, Crystal Lake
815/356-9212
www.rauecenter.org

Spend an evening enjoying fine Irish entertainment in this majestic performing arts theater. Don't miss their St. Patrick's Day production, which is scheduled for mid-March. Visit their Web site for details.

Schaumburg Prairie Center for the Arts Irish Family Festival

201 Schaumburg Court, Schaumburg
847/895-3600
www.prairiecenter.org

Visit their Web site for details and call for reservations.

The Milk Pail Restaurant's *When Irish Cows Are Smiling*

14 State Route 25, East Dundee
847/742-4041
www.themilkpail.com

This suburban banquet and entertainment complex presents a dinner show guaranteed to tickle your funny bone. This 90-minute audience-participation comedy is set in 1872, just after the Great Chicago Fire. Call for reservations.

Pub and Restaurant Events

Celtic Knot Public House

626 Church Street, Evanston

847/864-1679

www.celticknotpub.com

Live entertainment at this weeklong Hooley featuring traditional music sessions and céilí dancing. Call for details.

Duke O'Brien's

110 North Main Street, Crystal Lake

815/356-9980

www.dukeobriens.com

Enjoy a fun-packed evening inside their heated tent. Join in the St. Baggo Tournament while enjoying green beer, Irish music, dancers, great food and live band.

Durty Nellie's Pub

180 North Smith Street, Palatine

847/358-9150

Join in their weeklong St. Patrick's Day celebration party. And mark your calendars for the spring and fall beer festivals. This mega pub of Irish bars with multiple beer gardens and a rooftop terrace has good food and a huge beer selection and other great drinks.

Mickey Finn's

412 North Milwaukee Avenue, Libertyville

847/362-6688

www.mickeyfinnsbrewery.com

Party in the beer tent and enjoy all-day-long festivities. Look for Irish dancers, good entertainment and great craic.

Southwest Suburbs

Charity Benefits

O'Sullivan's Irish Pub's St. Baldrick's Fundraiser and St. Patrick's Day Parties

24205 West Lockport Street, Plainfield

815/436-4529

www.osullivans-pub.com

Their St. Baldrick's charitable event is always held the Friday before St. Patrick's Day. Bagpipers, bands, and silent auction—all under the big tent. And it doesn't end there. Go back on Saturday for their huge St. Patrick's Day party.

Church Events

St. Fabian's Church's Fundraiser and Irish Mass

8300 South Thomas, Bridgeview
708/594-7540
www.saint-fabian.org

They wear green, speak a wee bit of the Irish, and celebrate to benefit the Franciscan Outreach Ministry, an inner-city ministry for the homeless. This Irish Mass draws standing-room-only crowds. Music performances by premier musicians of the Archdiocese and other well-known vocalists introduce several new compositions. Call for details.

Entertainment

Gaelic Park's "Ireland on Parade" Week

6119 West 147th Street, Oak Forest
708/687-9323
www.chicagogaelicpark.org

Join in the "Ireland on Parade." These Irish host a weeklong event celebrating the music and dance of Ireland. Enjoy a multitude of festivities that include performances by local dance schools and an Irish soda bread competition. Doors open for nightly performances at 5:30. Other hours vary. Visit their Web site for details.

Governor's State University, Center for Performing Arts St. Patrick's Day Brunch

1 University Parkway, University Park
708/235-2222
www.centertickets.net

Their annual St. Paddy's Day event includes brunch and Irish dancers. Call for reservations.

Pub and Restaurant Events

115 Bourbon Street

3359 West 115th Street, Marionette Park
708/388-8881
www.115bourbonstreet.com

Live radio broadcasts, pipe and drum bands, performances of *Flanagan's Wake*. Call for information and make reservations for their dinner/theatre event.

Jack Desmond's Irish Pub

10339 South Ridgeland Avenue Chicago Ridge
708/857-7910
www.jackdesmonds.com

Doors open at 9 am. for Irish breakfast, Irish Soda bread contests, fundraisers, and free bus ride to South Side Irish Parade. Scheduled events include pub darts, Irish karaoke, Irish dancers, and bagpipes. The patio will be open, weather permitting. Visit their Web site for additional information.

Murphy's Pub, Palos Country Club

13100 Southwest Highway, Orland Park

708/448-6550

www.paloscountryclub.com

Pre-parade bash with Irish music, food, and drink specials. Irish brunch offered while you watch the South Side Irish parade on TV. Irish dancers, soda bread contest, live bands, and Irish D.J.

Quigley's

4010 West 111th Street, Oak Lawn

708/952-4774

Irish soda bread contest, Irish dancers, live bands, Irish traditional music, and a screening of the movie *The Quiet Man*. This place rocks the entire week before St. Paddy's Day.

Sam Maguire's Irish Pub and Restaurant

39 Orland Square Drive, Orland Park

708/460-1771

www.sammaguires.net

Entertainment indoors or a heated tent. Keg and Eggs breakfast includes round-trip bus ride for the South Side parade. Live broadcasts, pub trivia, karaoke, Texas Holdem Tournament and lots of good music. Call for details and bus reservations.

West Suburbs

Charity Benefits

The Irish Fellowship Club of Chicago St. Patrick's Day Dinner

815 25th Avenue, Bellwood

312/427-2926

www.irishfellowshipchicago.com

For over 100 years, this group has hosted an annual St. Patrick's Day Dinner. The evening begins with cocktails, followed by dinner and entertainment. Irish dancers perform along with a Pipe and Drum band. Call for reservations.

West Side Irish Organization's Emerald Dinner Dance

Naperville

630/853-9461

www.wsirish.org

Join in their annual Emerald Dinner Dance. Delicious Irish food served. Proceeds donated to charitable organizations throughout the city. Call for reservations.

Delectable Delights

Uncle Harry's of Wisconsin's Green River Floats

1453 West Lake Street, Addison
630/629-2356

Enjoy a bit of nostalgia when you wrap your lips around a glass of Green River Soda. Add to that a large scoop of vanilla ice cream for the taste treat of the year. This place sells more Green River floats on St. Paddy's Day than any other time of year, so get in line for yours and celebrate with a toast to all things green.

Entertainment

Morton Arboretum's Irish, Scottish, and Welsh Entertainment

4100 Illinois Route 52, Lisle
630/968-0074

They offer a number of free activities honoring Irish, Scottish, and Welsh cultures. Along with Celtic storytelling sessions, the performances include Irish dancers, Celtic bands, and pipe and drum music. Call or visit their Web site for details.

Noble Fool Theatricals *Flanagan's Wake*

4051 East Main Street (Route 64), St. Charles
630/584-6342
www.pheasantrun.com

Flanagan's Wake is the hilarious interactive Irish wake that's been running in Chicago for the past 11 years. Make your reservations so you can participate in this Irish wake.

The Arcada Theatre's Music and Dance Festival

105 East Main Street, St. Charles
630/587-8400
www.onestientertainment.com/arcada/arcada.htm

Their festival brings a whole line up of wonderful Irish music and dance. Call for reservations.

The Gilhooly Music and Comedy Show

White Fence Farm Banquet Hall
1776 Joliet Road, Lemont
708/361-6067
www.whitefencefarm.com

Join the Gilhoolys for an Irish Hooley afternoon. Sing, laugh, dance, and enjoy lively antics performed by this entertaining couple. Offered the week of St. Patrick's Day, call to reserve seats for luncheon and show.

Pub and Restaurant Events

Ballydoyle

5157 West Main Street, Downers Grove

630/969-0600

www.ballydoylepub.com

Begin the day at 8 am with a ribbon cutting to commemorate the first Guinness pour. Breakfast buffet, Irish dancers, traditional Irish music, and Celtic rockers. Contests and drawings take place throughout the day.

Emmett's Tavern & Brewing Co.

5200 Main Street, Downer's Grove

630/434-8500

www.emmettstavern.com

It's all about the beer! Order their March house drink specialty: Irish Dry Stout. And to appease the taste buds, you'll find the addition of beer in their marinades, grilled meats, soups, salads. Check out their special menu items on St. Patrick's Day.

Fitzgerald's Nightclub

6615 West Roosevelt Road, Berwyn

708/788-2118

www.fitzgeraldsnightclub.com

Why hire a babysitter when you can bring the kids? This family-friendly pub invites you to enjoy live music indoors and in a heated tent, Irish dancing, food, buffet of Guinness beef stew, corned beef and cabbage, and other Irish fare.

McNally's Traditional Irish Pub

201 East Main Street, St. Charles

630/513-6300

www.mcnallysirishpub.com

Join in celebration of the Mass at 11 am as part of the bar's seven-day fladgh. Irish dancers, bands, songs, and many more surprises. Call ahead to reserve.

Resources

The following phone numbers and Web sites will direct you to all scheduled events in the city and suburbs:

Chicago Centerstage:
WWW.CENTERSTAGECHICAGO.COM

Chicago Office of Tourism:
WWW.877CHICAGO.COM

Chicago Traveler:
WWW.CHICAGOTRAVELER.COM

Department of Cultural Affairs:
312/742-7529,
WWW.EGOV.CITYOFCHICAGO.ORG

Everything Irish in Chicago:
WWW.CHICAGOIRISH.ORG

Exploring Chicago:
WWW.CITYOFCHICAGO.ORG/TOURISM

Great Doings: WWW.GREATDOINGS.COM

Illinois Bureau of Tourism:
WWW.ENJOYILLINOIS.COM

Mayor's Office of Special Events:
312/744-3315, hot line 312/744-3315,
WWW.CITYOFCHICAGO.ORG/SPECIALEVENTS,
or WWW.CHICAGOEVENTS.COM

Metromix: WWW.METROMIX.COM

Events,
Festivals,
and Tourism

Guinness visits a local Irish festival.

You've no doubt exhausted the St. Paddy's Day list of things to do, and now you find yourself suffering from withdrawal for the sheer want of an Irish experience. Take heart, because you'll still get the flavor and the variety with Irish events occurring throughout the city, year round. Enjoy trolley tours of Irish neighborhoods, fire truck tours to the site of O'Leary's cottage (now the Chicago Fire Academy), pub crawls, James Joyce's Bloomsday celebrations, Irish festivals, and many more scheduled events to get you through the rest of the year. Even the Chicago White Sox host their Halfway to St. Patrick's Day event in September.

Don't forget to check out the activities at the Irish American Heritage Center, WWW.IRISHAMHC.COM, on the North Side, for their Irish school, cultural and educational programs, not to mention the music, the dance, the language, and the theater that goes on throughout the year. Gaelic Park, WWW.CHICAGOGAELICPARK.ORG, on the South Side, offers GAA games held on their huge campus, as well as music and dance, inside their lovely facilities. Visit their Web sites for additional information.

Annual Events and Festivals

January

Young Irish Fellowship Club's Pub Crawl

312/902-1943
www.youngirish.com

Participate in the Young Irish Fellowship Club's pub crawl in late January to kick off their "Forever Green" March event. Fee includes T-shirt, bus transportation between bars, and drink specials. Visit their Web site for information on other scheduled events such as happy hours, sporting outings, cultural outings, cruises on Lake Michigan, and trips to Ireland.

February

Catholic Charities' Pre-St. Patrick's Day Party

West Suburban Services
1400 South Austin Boulevard, Cicero
708/222-1491
www.catholiccharities.net

Join in their annual pre-St. Patrick's Day Party to raise funds for the New Hope Apartments Transitional Housing Program. The party features hearty appetizers, spirits, Irish music, and dancing, plus great raffle prizes. Held the last Friday in February. Tickets may be purchased in advance by calling the organization.

University of Chicago Folk Festival

Mandel Hall, 1135 East 57th Street
773/702-9793
www.uofcfolk.org

Enjoy traditional international music with roots in Ireland, blues, bluegrass, Cajun culture, Sweden, Macedonia, and more. Runs the first weekend in February. Call for details or visit their Web site.

March

Check out "Wearin' o' the Green" (Chapter 7).

April

Chicago Cultural Center

77 East Randolph Street
312/742-1190
www.chicagoneighborhoodtours.com

"Threads of Ireland" is scheduled to run at least three times a year, with both private engagements for groups who book with the city and then public ones

arranged in advance by the Department of Cultural Affairs. Visit their Web site for dates and times.

Chicago Rose of Tralee Ball

Ridge Country Club
10522 South California Avenue
773/239-3927
www.chicagoroseoftralee.com

The most anticipated Irish formal event of the year, featuring the best of Irish entertainment, Irish dancing, silent auction, and the crowning of Chicago's Rose of Tralee. Proceeds from this black-tie affair go to sending the Chicago Rose to Ireland as Chicago's Irish Ambassador in the International Rose of Tralee Festival.

O'Leary's Chicago Fire Truck Tours

312/287-6565
www.olearysfiretours.com

Provides an entertaining, fact-filled trip around the city aboard a genuine antique

O'Leary's Fire Truck Tours, Chicago.

fire truck. Focusing on the Chicago fire and its legacy, the tour includes stops at two authentic Chicago fire stations, Chicago's historic Watertower and Pumping Station. Call for reservations. Runs through October, weather permitting.

Southern Illinois Irish Festival

Carbondale
618/549-3090
www.silirishfest.org

Distance means nothing when it comes to a good Irish festival. This event runs the last weekend in April. Top performers grace the venue, along with traditional dance, storytellers, an Irish marketplace, good food, and lots of Irish beer. What more could you ask for? It's definitely worth the trip. Visit their Web site for additional information.

WhiskeyFest Chicago

Hyatt Regency Chicago
151 East Wacker Drive
312/239-4544
Hosted by *Malt Advocate* magazine (Emmaus, Pennsylvania 610/967-1083)

The bottle of whiskey is the Irish barometer—a special drink for special occasions, its solitary presence reserved for the top shelf. Reserve your spot at America's largest whiskey celebration and sample your favorites among more than 250 of the world's finest, rarest and most expensive whiskies, featuring top-of-the-line Irish whiskies: Bushmills, Connemara, Jameson, Knappogue Castle, and Midleton, along with the finest single-malt and blended whiskies of Scot-

land. The focus is on education. Distillery representatives will be on hand at the pouring booths to explain the production. Call *Malt Advocate* magazine for tickets.

And the education doesn't need to end when the whiskey reps leave town. Chief O'Neill's Irish Pub schedules a celebration of whiskey, food, song, and great fun to keep the party going. They've been known to host a pig roast infused with Bulleit Bourbon. Call 773/473-5263 for information.

May

Beer On The Pier

Navy Pier, Festival Hall A
600 East Grand Avenue
312/595-PIER
www.beeronthepier.com

Lots of Irish beer! Check their Web site for the date and be sure to mark your calendars. Admission includes beer sampling and all entertainment. This indoor event features hundreds of local, national and international beers. Tickets are available online. Don't delay, for they sell out fast.

Chicago Gaelic Park Irish Fest

6119 West 147th Street, Oak Forest
708/687-9323
www.chicagogaelicpark.org

Includes top Irish entertainment on five lively stages. Irish step dancers, céilí dancing, Irish dog breeders, Gaelic Football, Tug-o-War, Red Hair and Freckle Contest, puppet shows, magicians, jugglers and clowns, petting zoo.Irish Fest Mall, food, and refreshments make this festival one of the biggest and best. Runs during Memorial Day weekend. Visit their Web site for details.

Chicago History Museum Bars and Bootlegging Prohibition-Era Chicago Trolley Tour

1601 North Clark Street
312/642-4600
www.chicagohs.org

Get a taste of the speakeasies once owned, operated, or frequented by Bugs Moran and other infamous gangsters. Learn how the prohibition shaped Chicago and its image worldwide. Bars on this trolley tour include the Green Mill, O'Donovans, John Barleycorn, the Kerryman, and Emmit's. This is a one-day event, so call for reservations.

Fiddler's Picnic

University of Chicago Campus
5706 South University Avenue
www.uofcfolk.org

An afternoon of free food, a fiddling contest, a concert, and lots of jamming. Bring your instruments. Check their Web site for details.

June

Chicago Cultural Center

77 East Randolph Street
312/742-1190
www.chicagoneighborhoodtours.com

Travel with expert Herman Schell as he takes you to the Fire Academy, the place where Mrs. O'Leary's cow allegedly knocked over the lantern. Finish at the Chicago History Museum's "Great Chicago Fire" exhibit. Lunch included. Call for reservations.

Chicago Sister Cities Festival on Daley Plaza

312/744-8074
www.chicagosistercities.com

Galway is represented in CSCIP's Festival on Daley Plaza with beautiful crafts from Nuada, Irish dancing troupes, and student Irish music performances. Usually scheduled very early in the month. Check their Web site for dates and times.

Highland Games & Scottish Festival

Oak Brook Polo Grounds
700 Oak Brook Road, Oak Brook
708/447-5092
www.chicago-scots.org

Two-day celebration featuring heavy athletics, Rugby, traditional Scottish cuisine and drink, pipe band competitions, Celtic music and dancing, children's crafts, and many more activities. Visit their Web site for dates and times.

Sam Maguire's

39 Orland Square Drive, Orland Park
708/460-1771
www.sammaguires.net

Three-night festival from 9 pm until closing. This place rocks with bands, partygoers, and special events.

St. Mike's Annual Party in the Plaza

1633 North Cleveland Avenue
312/266-1445
www.st-mikes.org

Scores of bands take the stage throughout the weekend on the plaza outside of St. Michael's with lots of food and beer vendors. Trinity Irish Dancers are on hand to entertain along with other fine music offerings. This event coincides with the Annual Old Town Art Fair, so you can take in two events in one day. Visit their Web site for details.

Taste of Chicago

Grant Park
www.tasteofchicago.us

Wherever there's food, beer and good music, you'll find the Irish. Look for the Irish pub that serves fish and chips, Irish potatoes, and corned beef sandwiches. Traditional Irish music performers can be found at the International Pavilion. Check their schedule to locate the pub and to find dates and times for the music session.

Abbey Pub at the Taste of Chicago.

Bloomsday

June 16 is the day designated to celebrate the life and works of James Joyce. On June 16, 1904, writer James Joyce met his wife, Nora Barnacle, and immortalized the date in his monumental epic, *Ulysses*. Modern Joyce aficionados have designated June 16 "Bloomsday," a day set aside throughout the world to honor the great man and his controversial and thought-provoking works.

Celebrating Bloomsday at the Irish American Heritage Center.

Cliff Dwellers Club

200 South Michigan Avenue, Suite 22
312/922-8080
www.cliff-chicago.org

Be sure to check their Web site for scheduling. Steve Dietrich, Newberry Library specialist on Joyce's famed novel, is the master of ceremonies. Open to the public without admission, this annual event always generates a capacity audience. An optional dinner is available. Call for reservations.

Irish American Heritage Center

4626 South Knox Avenue
773/282-7035
www.irishamhc.com

Don't miss their *Rattlin' of the Joists* presentation. You can expect to hear authentic Irish accents with a sprinkling of Irish wit and humor as the life and work of Dublin's favorite son is remembered through readings and song. After the show, visit the Fifth Province Pub to enjoy good Irish food, brew, and entertainment.

Red Lion Pub

2446 North Lincoln Avenue
773/348-2695
www.collageproductions.info

Jeff Helgeson, playwright and Roosevelt University administrator/adjunct instructor, hosts an informative and entertaining evening featuring readings from James Joyce's *Ulysses*. You'll find Joyce memorabilia and photographs—just what is needed to add atmosphere reflective of the Joyce era. And for any Joyce aficionados interested in performing with the actors, writers, and scholars, bring along a copy of *Ulysses*. This might be your opportunity to be brought into the storyline.

July

Annual Midwest Fiddle Championship Finals

Welles Park
2333 West Sunnyside Avenue
Contest sponsored by Seman Violins,
WWW.SEMANVIOLINS.COM, through the Old Town School of Folk Music,
773/728-6000
www.oldtownschool.org

This is a contest for music teams, a fiddler, and a second lead player, which celebrates the diverse sounds of fiddling in the Midwest. Adult Team and Youth Division finalists winning earlier rounds play for prize money on the Chicago Folk and Roots Festival main stage. Preliminary rounds are in various locations in the Lincoln Square neighborhood before the festival. Call or check the Old Town School of Folk Music Web site for rules and details.

Arlington Heights Irish Festival

Arlington Heights Historical Museum
110 West Fremont Street, Arlington Heights
847/255-1225
www.ahpd.org/museum/irishfest

Don't miss their annual Hooley. This festival promises loads of fun, from the "Best Legs in a Kilt" contest to performances by the hottest pub bands in Chicago. Vendors will be on hand to sell Irish goods, including CDs, knitwear, books, jewelry, and other collectibles. Good food, good Irish music, and dancing all round out a wonderful weekend. Visit their Web site for dates and times in July.

Chicago History Museum

1601 North Clark Street
312/642-4600
www.chicagohistory.org

Sign up for their literary pub-crawl. Learn about Chicago's often-overshadowed literary history as you visit various pubs that served as haunts for some of the city's signature scribes. Call for date and time.

Irish American Heritage Center's Irish Festival

4626 North Knox Avenue
773/282-7035
www.irishamhc.com

This festival is sure to please anyone searching for a true Irish experience. Be sure to visit their library, museum, cultural, and genealogy areas. This "jewel" in the heart of the city is a testament to the dedication and hard work of the Irish and Irish Americans who work to preserve and share their rich culture and tradition. The weekend festival includes Irish dancing, live bands, contests, Irish vendors, homemade Irish food prepared in their own kitchen, an Irish folk tent, and children's activities. Their Fifth Province Pub will be opened all weekend long, so you'll be guaranteed good brew in a comfortable air-conditioned setting.

Don't miss this one. Usually scheduled to run in the middle of July. Visit their Web site for dates and times.

McNally's Annual Irish American Summerfest

201 East Main Street, St. Charles
630/513-6300
www.mcnallysirishpub.com

Irish meets German with their Guinness Bratwurst. Wrap your jaw around this taste sensation. Live music and family fun, plus outdoor and indoor activities. Traditional Irish food served inside with more casual faire available outside, under the tent. Visit their Web site for date and time.

St. Patrick visits a suburban Irish festival.

The World's Largest Block Party

Old St. Pat's Church
700 West Adams Street
312/648-1590
www.worldslargestblockparty.com

Brings together thousands of people throughout the Chicago area for an annual summer celebration. The mission is to gather good people, to foster volunteerism, and to form enriching social relationships, all while providing significant funding. The block party has become a major annual event for many young adults in Chicago. Visit their Web site for dates and times.

Taste of Lincoln Avenue

Wrightwood Neighbors Association
www.chicagoevents.com

Don't miss their Irish Eyes stage for internationally renowned recording stars. One of the largest neighborhood festivals in the region, featuring over 300 vendors. You'll sure to find Guinness and good craic. Visit their Web site for details.

August

Edison Park Fest

Edison Park Chamber of Commerce
773/631-0063
www.edisonpark.com

Edison Park is home to one of Chicago's strongest Irish American communities.

Go for the live music and the Taste of Edison Park, which includes O'Connor's Market and Deli, beer gardens, and arts and crafts, as well as Irish dancers. Visit their Web site for details.

Milwaukee Irish Festival

Henry W. Maier Festival Grounds
200 North Harbor Drive,
Milwaukee, Wisconsin
www.milwaukeeirishfest.com

You'll be happy you made the trip. It's so huge they have a sky ride to take you from end of the park to the other. This four-day festival includes Irish dance troupes, top entertainers on numerous stages, a cultural area showcasing the Hedge School and an author corner, marketplace vendors, and genealogy experts. They offer a large variety of ethnic foods, drinks, and ice cream—just like an old-fashioned fair. Their tug-o-war teams battle daily on the grassy area alongside the cultural tents, and currach races are scheduled daily. Usually held the third weekend in August. Visit their Web site for dates and times.

Peggy Kinnane's Annual Golf Outing and Fundraiser

8 North Vail Avenue,
Arlington Heights
847/577-7733
www.peggykinnanes.com

Join in a round of golf after a hearty buffet breakfast. Beer will be provided at designated holes, and shot girls will be on the course. Prizes for longest drive, closest to the pin, longest putt, and best combined score. Visit their Web site for information.

Peoria Irish Festival

Water Street and Hamilton Blvd., Peoria
www.stpatpeoria.com

Plan to spend the weekend. This Irish extravaganza runs for three days, beginning on Friday afternoon and winding down on Sunday night. You'll not want to miss the music performances, Children's area, traditional Irish dance, Irish marketplace, cultural tent, music school, and good Irish food and brew. Usually held the last weekend in August, check their Web site for exact dates and times.

September

Half Way to St. Paddy's Day parties have become popular, so check with your favorite pub/restaurant to see if they are planning such an event.

Celtic Festival

Grant Park
300 South Columbus Drive
www.celticfestchicago.com

Usually scheduled for the second weekend in September, this fest includes dancing, music, entertainment, Celtic kids' area, Celtic Voice Tent, Harp Tent, Next Generation Tent, Uilleann Pipe Tional, and other Celtic activities/performers.

Chicago White Sox Halfway to St. Patrick's Day

U.S. Cellular Field
312/559-1212 (Ticketmaster), 866/SOX-GAME.
www.whitesox.com

This annual event is a celebration of Chicago's rich Irish heritage. The White Sox wear green pinstriped uniforms and green caps designed especially for this event. The evening's entertainment includes Irish bands, dance troupes and bagpipers throughout the ballpark. Order your tickets and join the party.

Eli's Cheesecake Festival

6701 West Forest Preserve Avenue
773/205-3800
www.elicheesecake.com

You'll find Trinity Irish Dancers and lots of great cheesecake. And you might just be able to sample their Baileys Cheesecake. Now that's worth the drive.

Fox Valley Folk Music & Storytelling Festival

Island Park, Geneva
www.foxvalleyfolkmusicfestival.com

Usually held the first weekend in September. Live music, including bluegrass, by Irish and Scottish groups. Eight stage areas, old-time community barn dance, ghost stories, and storytelling workshops. Bring your own instruments for hands-on workshops and jamming. Camping available three blocks from Chicago and Northwestern Metra Railroad. Festival runs rain or shine. Visit their Web site for additional information.

Galway Tribes Irish Pub

9680 Lincolnway Lane, Frankfort
815/464-9881

If you enjoy oysters with your Guinness, get yourself to this tasty event. Their annual Oyster and Music Festival is usually scheduled for the middle of the month, but call for dates and times; you'll not want to miss out on this event. Oyster cooking demos and eating contests are not to be missed. Instruments are always on hand in case a session breaks out without warning.

Guinness Oyster Festival

2000 West Roscoe Street
773/868-3010
www.chicagoevents.com

Annual fete features fresh-shucked oysters, live music, on two stages, and food vendors, plus pints of Guinness and Harp. Visit their Web site for dates and time.

Irish Mill Inn's St. Patrick's Day Practice Party

26592 North IL-83, Mundelein
847/566-7044
www.irishmillinn.com

It's never too early to begin preparations for St. Patrick's Day, and what better way than with a St. Patrick's Day Practice

Party, a Saturday event chock full of music, Irish food, Irish dancers, and entertainment for the wee little ones. Definitely worth the trip; you'll find a friendly neighborhood atmosphere. Visit their Web site for additional events to be scheduled during the year.

Long Grove Irish Days

228 Robert Parker Coffin Road, Long Grove
847/634-0339
www.irishboutique.com

Three days of all things Irish—food, entertainment, and folk and heritage events—for the entire family. Don't miss the "Best Looking Men's Legs in a Kilt Contest!" Paddy and John Barry schedule the finest entertainment this side of Dublin with Champion Irish dancers, bagpipers, Irish dog competitions, traditional as well as contemporary Irish music, marketplace vendors, good food, a variety of libations and a friendly atmosphere. Usually runs during Labor Day weekend. Visit their Web site for details.

Blarney Irish Shop at a local festival.

Midlothian Scottish Fair

Village Green, 147th and Springfield Avenue, Midlothian
708/389-0200
www.villageofmidlothian.net

Held on the last Saturday in September. Entertainment includes several kinds of dancing—Irish, Scottish Highland Scottish country—pipe bands, fiddle competitions, sheep herding, vendors, storytellers, children's activities, and lots of good food and brew. No cost for admission, free parking.

Misericordia Family Fest

6300 North Ridge Avenue
773/973-6300
www.misericordia.com

Sister Rosemary knows how to throw a party. You'll find an entire tent set up just for Irish activities—music, dancing, delicious Irish food, and great company. Scheduled for the Sunday after Labor Day.

Old St. Pat's Church

700 West Adams Street,
312/831-9355
www.oldstpats.org

Join members and their friends for a delightful evening of dinner and dancing at the Emerald Ball. Call for reservations.

O'Sullivan's Irish Pub

24205 West Lockport Street, Plainfield
815/436-4529
www.osullivans-pub.com

Mark your calendars for this Halfway to St. Paddy's Day Party to benefit Cancer Research for Kids. There'll be an outside tent with festivities from noon to midnight.

St. Catherine's Irish Fest

845 West Main Street, Dundee
www.stcatherinesirishfest.com

Bookmark your calendars for the second weekend in September. Performance from Irish dancing schools, shopping at the Irish marketplace, food from local vendors, pipe bands, singers, entertainers, children's area, and a raffle. Don't miss this last festival of the summer. Visit their Web site for details.

The Gilhooly Travelin' Show

708/361-6067

Sign up for the Halfway to St. Patrick's Day Party at the Irish Cottage Hotel in historic Galena. Fully escorted by Paddy & Kathleen Gilhooly with North & South Side pickup. Call to book reservations.

October

Chicago Cultural Center

77 East Randolph Street
312/742-1190
www.chicagoneighborhoodtours.com

Learn about the myths and facts of one of the most celebrated disasters in American history, the Great Chicago Fire of 1871. The tour begins at Mrs. O'Leary's homestead, now the home of the Chicago Fire Academy. This modern building is where firefighters are trained. The tour continues on the inferno's path and visits the Chicago History Museum's permanent Great Chicago Fire Exhibit. This tour runs only one day out of the year, so be sure and book early. Call or visit their Web site for details.

For teachers: The Great Chicago Fire: Did Mrs. O'Leary's Cow Really Cause It?

Education-World, WWW.EDUCATION-WORLD.COM (search subjects under "History" then scroll down to "Chicago Fire")

Connor Clarke celebrates his Irish in grand style.

For all educators interested in teaching a fire safety curriculum for Fire Safety Week, you'll find lessons for grades 6 through 12.

St. Casimir/Mt. Olivet Cemetery

4401 West 111th Street,
Mt. Greenwood
773/238-4435
www.findagrave.com

Visitors come during Fire Prevention Month to visit Mrs. O'Leary's gravesite. Stop at St. Casimir's to obtain a map. They will direct you to Mt. Olivet, where you'll find the tombstone. Open all year long.

Did the Cow Do It?

Richard F. Bales
www.thechicagofire.com

Chicago attorney, Richard Bales, author of the book, *The Great Chicago Fire and the Myths of Mrs. O'Leary's Cow*, published in 2002 by McFarland and Company, gives a whole new look at the cause of the Great Chicago Fire.

The Gilhooly Travelin' Show

708/361-6067

Hop on Gilhooly's Jolly Bus for a trip to the Irish Cottage in Galena, where you'll enjoy their Irish-themed show filled with song, dance, and merriment. Fully escorted tour by Paddy and Kathleen Gilhooly. Call for reservations.

November

Chicago Rose of Tralee Fashion Show

773/239-3927
www.chicagoroseoftralee.com

Your opportunity to view an Irish fashion show titled "The Little Known History of Irish Courtier." Proceeds benefit breast cancer research.

Decorate the Irish Tree at the Museum of Science and Industry

Irish American Heritage Center
4626 North Knox Avenue
773/282-7035
www.irishamhc.com

Join members of the IAHC to decorate the Irish-themed Christmas tree at the Science and Industry Museum. For over 60 years, the museum has held its "Christmas Around the World," exhibit featuring decorated trees representing countries around the globe. To join the fun, contact Kathy Mahoney at IAHC, or E-mail SULLY101@YAHOO.COM

The Galway Committee of the Chicago Sister Cities International Program

312/744-8074
amy.oconnor@cityofchicago.org

This organization hosts their annual Oyster Festival at Hawthorne Race Course in Cicero. All proceeds benefit the Galway Committee of the CSCIP. Join in the fun for lunch, live thoroughbred racing, Irish entertainment, and raffle prizes. Call or E-mail Amy O'Connor for tickets.

December

Irish American Heritage Center's Irish Mass, Irish Breakfast, and Christmas Market

4626 North Knox Avenue
773/282-7035
www.irishamhc.com

Begin the day with an Irish Mass and a hearty Irish breakfast. This will set the mood for some Christmas shopping. Beautifully crafted Irish handwork, Irish-themed gifts, books, bakery selections, etc., all available at the IAHC. This is your one-stop shopping for those hard to find gifts. Call for reservations for the Irish breakfast.

Travel and Tourism

Irish Sites

St. James at Sag Bridge Church and Cemetery

Lemont
www.canalheritage.com

Irish immigrants working on the Illinois and Michigan Canal founded St. James Catholic Church at Sag Bridge. During the nineteenth century the Irish custom was to inscribe the county and parish of origin on the gravestones. Visit the cemetery and read the old gravestones, or visit their Web site and click on the link for a list of places and names found on gravestones. Obituaries and gleanings taken from old newspapers have been added to their Web site as well.

The Irish Castle

10244 South Longwood Drive
773/233-7080
www.beverlyunitarian.org

Registered at the Smithsonian Institution as an historical landmark, the Irish Castle was built in 1886 by Robert G. Givens. It replicated an existing ivy-covered estate on the River Dee, between Belfast and Dublin, in his ancestral Ireland. Stories reveal that it was a romantic surprise for his bride. Now home to the Beverly Unitarian Church. Rooms are available to rent for weddings, receptions, family functions, banquets, seminars, classes, and meetings.

Chicago's Irish Castle.

Irish Lodging

Innisfree Celtic Bed & Breakfast

702 West Colfax Avenue, South Bend, Indiana
574/283-0740
www.innisfreebnb.com

Plan your getaway at this lovely Irish-themed B & B. You'll be entertained by traditional Irish bands, participate in karaoke, beat the bodhrán, and even dance a jig. And for you football fans, Notre Dame home game Thursdays run from late August through November.

The Irish Cottage Boutique Hotel

9853 U.S. Highway 20, Galena
866/284-7474
www.TheIrishCottage.com

If you're up for the drive (160 miles northwest of Chicago) and are looking for a true Irish experience, you'll want to book this hotel. Nestled on 20 acres, this hotel is a tribute to Irish craftsmanship. The sights, sounds, and smells of the Motherland envelop you the moment you enter the front door. The décor of the lobby, the W.B. Yeats Library, and the Frank O'Dowd's Irish Pub feature rich oaks and mahoganies, stained glass, and exquisite tile, all of which were handcrafted in Ireland and painstakingly reassembled in Galena. Each of their guestrooms is individually themed for a county in Ireland.

Irish Cruises and Tour Packages

The Irish Festival Cruise

Celebrity Cruise Line's Millennium
800/441-HARP
www.irishtours.com/cruise.html

If you've thought of planning an Irish-themed anniversary or honeymoon, this is just the ticket. Their cruise leaves out of Fort Lauderdale, Florida. Join them as they mingle Celtic and Caribbean flavors on a tropical Hooley. You can practice the jig, a reel, the hornpipe, or learn to play the tin whistle. Tackle some conversational Gaelic to astound your friends and confound your enemies. This trip offers you the Irish music

you love so well. Delight in over 40 hours of Irish entertainment throughout the week. Take in Irish theater and learn about the bodhrán or Celtic mythology. There's golf, shuffleboard, dancing, and a pool. Visit their Web site for booking information.

All Star Irish Caribbean and Mediterranean Charter Cruises

Gertrude Byrne Promotions
P.O. Box 6, Leeds, New York, 81019
800/356-4713
www.gertrudebyrnepromotions.com

Get on board this all-Irish cruise with Ireland's greatest entertainers, and experience a magical and breathtaking journey. The entire ship is dedicated to this Irish cruise. From the traditional Irish breakfast to the Irish musicians and entertainers, this cruise is sure to please. They sell out quickly so book early. Visit their Web site for additional information.

Andy Cooney's Cruise of Irish Stars

800/499-2010
www.cruiseofirishstars.com

Sail from Fort Lauderdale to the Western Caribbean or to the Eastern Caribbean. These seven-night cruises include Irish dance classes, daily Mass, and a variety of Irish entertainment.

Seven Drunken Nights Tour of Ireland

Celtic tours and MAC Travel

847/344-2364

**mactravel@consultant.com,
www.celticratpack.com**

The Larkin and Moran Brothers invite you to join them on their sightseeing tour of Ireland. See the sights, sing the songs, and visit the Cliffs of Mohr, Connemara, the Ring of Kerry, Blarney Castle, and more. Call for booking information.

Shopping

Chicago's favorite, Maureen O'Looney
(left) outside her shop with Bonnie Shea.

You don't have to travel all the way to Ireland to surround yourself with treasures from the Emerald Isle — it's all here in Chicago. From the delicate Belleek Parian China to the lovely knitted sweaters and capes, Irish stores in the Chicago area offer a multitude of fine Irish goods.

If you're planning a trip to Ireland, consider purchasing souvenirs at your local store. Not only will you save money but you'll also avoid the hassle of squeezing everything into your already over-stuffed suitcases. If you have goods shipped from Ireland, you'll be left wondering when they'll arrive and in what condition. Purchasing souvenirs and gifts at home just makes sense and provides more time to spend exploring and appreciating the beauty, culture, and history of Ireland, instead of prowling through souvenir shops looking for those special gifts for Aunt Jane, Uncle Harry, and the kids.

Many of Chicago's Irish specialty stores sell the popular foods, so you'll be able to re-create those delicious Irish breakfasts enjoyed at all the hotels and B&Bs — including the black and white pudding.

I've listed a few Irish shops in the different neighborhoods of the city and suburbs. Many stores stock an impressive array of Irish music CDs, cassettes, records, books, clothing (including Irish dance shoes), religious articles, fire and police Irish-themed items, fine art, Belleek china, Tara, Galway crystal, T-shirts, Irish jewelry and lovely pottery from the various counties of Ireland. You'll also find Irish food markets, bakeries and delis. Call the shops to inquire about specific items of interest. Shop here at home and save your Ireland trip for sightseeing.

Irish Shops

Chicago: Downtown

Gift Shops and Boutiques

Teahan's

Navy Pier
600 East Grand Avenue
773/637-3800
www.irishimportschicago.com

Great selection of Irish clothing, baby items, jewelry, books, Irish CDs, and a wide variety of all things Irish for those must-have items. This is the place to shop for your antique Belleek China pieces with the black stamp imprint. Their other store is located on North Harlem Avenue.

The Illinois Artisans Shop

James R. Thompson Center
100 West Randolph Street, Suite 2-200
312/814-5321

Fine crafted lithographed St. Patrick's Day cards, woodcarvings of Celtic designs from the Book of Kells, cloth dolls, and a variety of other items available for purchase.

Chicago: North Side

Gift Shops and Boutiques

Donegal Imports

5358 West Devon Avenue
773/792-2377
www.donegalimports.com

Beautiful selection of fine china and crystal. Check out their lovely wool cardigans, caps, shawls, and blankets, T-shirts and other Irish gifts.

Gaelic Imports

6346 West Gunnison Street
773/792-1905

Most of Ireland's county newspapers can be purchased here every Tuesday morning, along with Ireland's Sunday papers as well as the Irish Echo from New York. Place your order while you shop in their lovely gift store.

Shamrock Imports

3150 North Laramie Avenue
773/286-6866

Maureen O'Looney keeps busy, because not only does she run this lovely Irish gift shop, she also hosts a Wednesday evening radio show on WSBC, 1240 AM. Charming and gracious, Maureen greets each shopper with her winning smile as she happily provides the inside scoop to whom and what's Irish in Chicago. In business over 40 years, her store is stocked with lovely Irish gifts at excellent prices. You'll even find Irish newspapers.

Teahan's

2505 North Harlem Avenue
773/637-3800
www.irishimportschicago.com

Opened over 45 years ago. Mary Rose Teahan stocks a wonderful selection of lovely Irish products, including clothing, baby items, jewelry, books, Irish CDs, and a wide variety of all things Irish for those must have items. This is the place to shop for your antique Belleek China pieces imprinted with the black stamp.

Trinity & Shamrock

7331 North Harlem Avenue
847/647-7774
www.trinityirishgifts.com

Specializing in religious goods, this lovely store provides First Communion gifts, Confirmation keepsakes, bibles, holy cards, and pictures. They also carry a unique and lovely collection of Irish gifts and apparel. Visit their satellite store at Navy Pier.

Food Markets

O'Connor's Deli & Market

7280 West Devon Avenue
773/631-0747
www.oconnorsdeli.com

Features a complete line of Irish groceries, candies, homemade soda bread, brown bread and scones, homemade shepherd's pie, sausage rolls, and much more. They also provide daily lunch and dinner specials with homemade soups and salads.

Fine Arts and Specialty Stores

Nuada, Chicago's Gallery of Contemporary Celtic Art and Design

773/525-4200
info@nuada.com, www.NUADA.com

Nuada is about beauty in design and craftsmanship. They offer unique artwork, jewelry, home decor items, and accessories created by a new generation of visionary artists. Each piece reflects the highest standards of beauty, design, and craftsmanship.

Nuada at the Taste of Chicago.

Chicago: South Side

Gift Shops and Boutiques

South Side Irish Imports

3446 West 111th Street
773/881-8585

You'll be impressed with their fine selection of clothing, books, CDs, crystal, china, baby gifts,

and cards. Parking is available right outside their door. Visit their other fine store in Tinley Park.

Food Markets

Winston's Market

4791 West 63rd Street
773/767-4353

Full line of imported Irish food, their product is also available at fine Irish shops throughout Chicago and suburbs. Irish sausage, black and white pudding, soda bread prepared fresh daily. Location in Tinley Park, as well.

Music

Beverly Records

11612 South Western Avenue
773/779-0066
www.beverlyrecords.com

Sellers of traditional and contemporary Irish music on CDs, cassettes, and LPs. The South Side Irish song is available on a 45-RPM kelly-green vinyl record, perfect for the jukebox or record player. Sounds like the perfect collector piece.

Northwest Suburbs

Gift Shops and Boutiques

Blarney, Fine Irish Jewelry

800/788-7429
www.blarneyhome.com

Lovely selection of Celtic wedding bands in 10k, 14k, 18k yellow and white gold and platinum. You'll find engagement rings and precious and semi-precious stone settings, as well as a large selection of necklaces, bracelets, and charms. From babies to brides, Blarney Fine Jewelry is the place to buy that special gift for someone you love. Located in the Northwest suburbs. Visit their Web site and call for information.

Paddy's On The Square, Long Grove.

Irish Connoisseur

1232 Waukegan Road, Glenview
847/998-1988

Purchase Irish gifts as well as the favorite foods of Ireland. Lovely store to browse and pick up all those gifts you'll need for special occasions.

Paddy's On The Square

228 Coffin Road, Long Grove
847/634-0339
www.irishboutique.com

Paddy Barry, Paddy's On The Square, Long Grove.

The Irish Boutique

434 Coffin Road, Long Grove
847/634-3540

The Irish Boutique

Crystal Lake Plaza
6600 Northwest Hwy, Crystal Lake
815/459-1800

The Irish Boutique

Woodfield Mall Kiosk
847/969-0166

Patrick and John Barry offer shoppers four locations. In each of their stores you'll find quality gifts from Ireland at great prices. Paddy's Irish and Celtic CD selection is unrivalled in breadth and quality. The two-story Irish emporium at the main store at 228 Coffin Road includes fine art and children's and adult clothing, official Guinness licensed products and barware collection, fine Irish crystal, and china and pottery, as well as a large variety of Irish-themed gift selections. Browse their second-floor library and purchase some of the finest Irish books available, along with Irish woolens, tweed caps, blankets, and fisherman knit sweaters.

Their Irish Boutiques stock everything else from Ireland that couldn't fit inside of Paddy's on the Square, including a wide variety of Irish food. And be sure to visit their kiosk at Woodfield Mall for a fine sampling of quality crafted goods.

Bakeries and Delis

Clarke's Bakery and Deli

455 West Northwest Highway, Barrington

847/381-5113

Great selection of delicious treats to satisfy your sugar craving. They specialize in wedding cakes, specialty cakes, and sweet tables. And if you're looking for a good Irish breakfast without the pub atmosphere, look no further. Clarke's offers a full Irish breakfast as well as a lunch and dinner menu. They stock a selection of Cadbury chocolates, including Flakes, Maltesers, Boland's Elite Chocolate Pies, and Kimerlys. You can wash it all down with a Guinness, Harp or Smithwicks, as well as domestic beer and wine.

Galway Bakers

259 South Park Avenue, Wheeling

847/813-5159

The specialty breads are to die for, and you'll be amazed at the variety of delicious sweets. Treat yourself to a bag of Irish goodies; I promise you'll leave smiling. Call to enroll in their Irish traditional baking classes in the kitchen on Saturday afternoons. They will teach the traditional way to make a variety of soda breads, pies, scones, and more.

Southwest Suburbs

Gift Shops and Boutiques

A Touch of Ireland

6761 West 95th Street, Oak Lawn

708/237-3473

St. James Crossing Mall, 808 East Ogden Avenue, Westmont

630/325-6200

www.touchofireland.com

Two lovely stores where you can shop for that special gift, they specialize in gifts for weddings, religious occasions, graduations, and birthdays. Don't miss their selection of custom-designed T-shirts, Irish dancewear, and a variety of fine-crafted Irish goods. They stock Winston's food products.

Touch of Ireland, Oak Lawn.

Celtic Cottage

12244 South Harlem Avenue, Palos Heights

708/361-8800

www.celticcottagedirect.com

Specializing in fine china and crystal, as well as books, CDs, clothing, and T-shirts. Your one-stop shopping place for all things Irish.

Murray's Irish Outfitters

The Oak Brook Promenade
3021 Butterfield Road, Oak Brook
630/572-1520

Chicagoland's premier Irish store. Leaders in Irish sportswear.

South Side Irish Imports

7725 West 159th Street, Tinley Park
708/444-4747

Shop their location on 111th Street in Chicago as well. Lovely store stocked full of Irish gifts from children's ware, books, and CDs to fine crystal and china.

Fine Arts and Specialty Stores

Tim McCarthy Fine Arts

3354 West 95th Street, Evergreen Park
708/636-5711
tim@mccarthyfinearts.com,
www.mccarthyfinearts.com

Step into this studio to view beautiful Irish-themed watercolors. Bring in a picture of your family's Irish cottage in Ireland or any of your favorite photos, and Tim will recreate it in watercolor, oils, or pencil. Besides creating fabulous artwork, Tim is a full-time Chicago fireman. Visit his Web site for additional information.

G&L Chicago Firefighter and Cop Shop

4038 West 111th Street, Oak Lawn
708/425-2884
www.chicagofireandcopshop.com

Specializing in items of interest to all city firemen and police. Besides the usual firefighter and police gear, you can also purchase Irish decals imprinted with *Men of Fire* in the Irish language with the English translation. They also carry T-shirts printed with *Fighting Irish Garda* for police. Visit their Web site for additional information on their Irish-themed products.

Food Markets

Winston's Market

7959 West 159th Street, Tinley Park
708/633-7500

The very best in Irish cuisine. Irish sausage, black and white pudding, soda bread, bacon prepared fresh each day, and they ship anywhere in the U.S. The majority of the food products sold in the Irish shops come from Winston's. Chicago location as well.

Bakeries and Delis

Bit O'Bread

17216 Oak Park Avenue, Tinley Park
708/614-9474

Cozy up with a cup of tea and a few slices of fresh-baked Irish soda bread, and stay to watch the bakers. There are no partitions between the dining area and the bakeshop, thus providing the perfect opportunity to watch the master at work. Lots of specialty items, including great tasting muffins. If you're looking for that special Irish party favor, they'll whip up miniature Irish soda loaves wrapped with festive colored ribbons and attach a tea bag—the perfect addition to wedding showers, baby showers, or any occasion.

West Suburbs

Gift Shops and Boutiques

A Touch of Ireland

5151 Main Street, Downers Grove
630/352-1952

Features Waterford crystal, Belleek china, Guinness apparel, and everything Irish.

Irish Sisters

312 South Third Street, Geneva
630/208-9300

Lovely Irish gifts, including woolen goods, Belleek china, Guinness products, and jewelry.

Irish Treasure Trove, Ltd.

138 North York Terrace, Elmhurst
630/530-2522

From Guinness and Notre Dame gear to traditional Irish sweaters, Irish dance apparel, Waterford glassware, and Belleek china dishes and accents.

The Irish Shop

100 Nort Oak Park Avenue, Oak Park
708/445-1149

Celtic finery includes wool sweaters and jackets, Irish step shoes, Belleek china, and Claddagh jewelry.

The Irish Way

105 West Jefferson Avenue, Naperville
630/778-8657

Irish specialty shop featuring furniture and home furnishings, novelty clothing, silver collectibles, and more.

Florists

Irish Garden

8863 Burlington Avenue, Brookfield
708/680-5024

Flowers and balloon arrangements, funeral flowers, wedding flowers, all-occasion bouquets, and custom jewelry. Call for more information.

Internet Shopping

Browse from your easy chair, click to order, and you're all set. I've listed a variety of specialty stores you'll want to take a look at. Although not all of them are located in the Chicago area, they guarantee quick and safe delivery.

Apparel and Flags

Maureen@meaden.com

708/301-1587

Aran sweaters hand-knit by Maureen Neylon.

ShopIrish.com

Irish flags, gifts, jewelry, clothing, music, books, and more.

Food

Many ingredients in Irish cooking are available at any local grocery store. However, a few things can only be purchased at specialty stores. Items such as bangers, Irish bacon, black and white pudding, Barry's tea—are you craving anything yet? If so, then read on, visit the Web sites and order up the grub.

www.celticbrands.com

Your online grocery store for traditional favorite foods of Ireland, including Irish breakfast specialties, tea, cookies, biscuits, candy, Taytos, and holiday goodies.

www.IrishGrub.com

Owner Bernard Kavanagh guarantees all his products are "the real thing." The company is located in California but ships nationwide.

www.foodireland.com

Shop their huge selection from Irish cookies or biscuits to beverages, Irish tea, and Irish sodas, from the vast selection of Irish candy or sweets to cereal, potato chips, dessert items, and their Home Cooking line, which has every item you need to whip up a traditional Irish meal. They specialize in fresh Irish smoked salmon, Irish butter and dairy spreads, and imported Irish cheeses.

www.KerryGold.com

825 Green Bay Road, Wilmette
847/256-8289:

Check out this Web site for information on Irish butter and cheese selections. Kerrygold products are available at major supermarkets, specialty shops, pubs, and restaurants. Also at Irish gift shops throughout Chicago.

www.tommymoloneys.com

A taste of home, Tommy provides lovely Irish breakfast gift baskets, fresh salmon, and other delicious Iris delicacies. Call toll free 800/431-6365.

Canines

Irish Terrier.

The Emerald Isle has brought us a wonderful selection of dogs. Back in the time of St. Patrick, breeds such as the water spaniel, the wolfhound, and the beagle were reserved for nobility, and commoners had to be content with terriers. Now, Irish breeds have become quite popular all over the world.

There are nine native breeds of dog from Ireland, four Terriers, two Hounds, and three Gundogs. In the 1840s, around the time of the Great Famine, there was not the luxury of owning different dogs for different tasks. The common dogs of Ireland had to be hardy and practical. They had to be herders, guards, pest controllers, hunters, companions, and, most of all, economical to feed and keep.

Contact the American Kennel Association (www.ack.org) in your area for breeders and clubs, as well as rescue resources. Adopt a lovely Irish dog, because after the parades, the parties, the festivals, and the music sessions, it sure is good to relax in your favorite easy chair in front of the hearth with an affectionate cold snoot in your lap. There's an old Irish saying that a dog has more friends because he wags his tail instead of his tongue. Is it any wonder there are so many Irish breeds?

Irish Dog Breeds

Irish Glen of Imaal Terrier

A small Corgi-type dog with bowed forequarters and a wiry, shaggy coat. The breed originated in Wicklow, Ireland, and was developed as a working terrier, proficient in hunting badger and fox. Glens adore human contact and are good with children. For a list of recommended breeders, visit the Clan of Imaal Terrier Club of America at WWW.GLENS.ORG. E-mail Noreen O'More at GITCACS@YAHOO.COM.

Irish Setters

Everybody's darlings. Also known as Red Setters, their coats are moderately long and silky and of a deep red color. They were originally bred for hunting, specifically for pointing game birds. Their refined and dignified look makes them hard to pass without a second glance. They are friendly, playful, and active and they love human contact and are excellent with children. Not recommended for inactive families or apartment dwellers. Contact Irish Setter Club of America, www.irishsetterclub.org, for information. E-mail Fran Sloughfy at SLOUGHFYE@AOL.COM.

Irish Red and White Setter

Virtually identical in use and temperament to its cousin, the Irish setter, but is more often found as a working dog. The coat is long and silky, mostly white, with deep red patches. For many years breeders developed only the red varieties, almost bringing the breed to extinction. Contact Irish Red and White Setter Association, Inc.,

WWW.IRISHREDWHITESETTERASSOCIATION.COM.
E-mail Kathy Pellerito at KPIRWSA@MSN.COM.

Irish Terriers

They look like a cross between an Airedale and a wirehaired fox terrier. This is a true breed that has been around for about 2,000 years. Bushy eyebrows and a reddish-colored coat give Irish terriers a Celtic look, which is fitting for these affectionate dogs. Contact the Irish Terrier Club of Chicago, WWW.IRISHTERRIERS.COM/ITCC.HTM. E-mail Gayle Cummings at TERRIER.ITCA@VERIZON.NET.

Irish Water Spaniels

The look of a medieval nobleman in dog form. Fine looking, curly-coated canines, they're strongly built, with characteristically long ratlike hairless tails that are a striking contrast to their otherwise curly coats. Extremely intelligent and inquisitive, they can also be shy and independent. They share a common lineage with the poodle and Portuguese water dog. Developed in Ireland in the 1830s. Contact the Irish Water Spaniel Club of America, clubs.akc.org/iwsc/.

Irish Wolfhounds

Known as the "Irish Dogs." They are so striking in their appearance that, once seen, they are rarely forgotten. Officially the tallest dog in the world, they can reach 7 feet when standing on their hind legs. Their astonishing size, speed, intelligence, and amiable nature once made them ideal for hunting deer and wolves. These gentle giants make great house pets. Contact the Great Lakes Irish wolfhound Association, WWW.IWCLUBOFAMERICA.ORG. E-mail Judith Simon at STONEYBROOKJUDY@AOL.COM.

Kerry Beagle

One of the most ancient breeds of Irish dogs. They are really not beagles at all but a are variety of foxhound found in Ireland. There are probably no Kerry beagles in this country, unless imported and incorporated into one of the organized fox hunting packs. So what some might call a Kerry Beagle might be just a dark blue tricolor beagle. Not officially recognized by the AKC, the Kerry Beagle is quite popular in the far west of County Kerry, Ireland.

Kerry Blue

These puppies are born black. The blue appears gradually when they're about two years old. Used for hunting, cattle herding, and guarding, they make great companions because of their intelligence. Michael Collins, one of the most active and noteworthy leaders in Irish history, was an owner and exhibitor of Irish blue terriers. His dog, Convict 224, competed for the Wyndham Quinn trophy in October 1920.

Kerry Blue.

Michael Collins did sponsor an Act of Parliament to elevate the Irish blue to the status of national dog of Ireland; however, there is no record of this legislation being passed. The fact that the legislation was presented is for many people the proof of the Kerry Blue's national status. Contact the Great Lakes All Terrier Association, Kerry Blue Terrier Club of Chicago, www.chicagokerryblues.org. E-mail Ellen Burrows at EME576@HOTMAIL.COM

Soft-Coated Wheaten Terriers

A history firmly rooted in Irish soil. Originally bred as working dogs to hunt game and to guard home and stock, this terrier has evolved to be a much-sought-after family pet. Their soft, infrequently shedding coat is wheat-colored, with occasional black, white, or darker brown markings. They are less aggressive and less stubborn in nature than that of other terrier breeds. Their temperament is curious, friendly, and very sociable.

Contact WWW.SCWTCA.ORG. E-mail Barbara Zapf at REDHILLWHEEATENS@ADELLPHIA.NET

Border Collie

Not officially identified as an Irish dog, but you'll find them throughout Ireland. For over 200 years they've been used primarily for sheep herding and can be seen to this day running through the fields or walking along the country roads. Extremely intelligent, these dogs make great pets, as they are loyal. Be sure you get these beautiful dogs out of the house every day for some good exercise with a Frisbee toss or two; they are quite active. Contact WWW.BORDERCOLLIESOCIETY.COM. E-mail Terri Clingerman at TACDOGS@REDSUSPENDERS.COM.

Emmy the Border Collie.

Soft-Coated Wheaten Terrier puppy.

Citizenship
and
Genealogy

*Foreign Birth Registry Document,
Irish/United States Passports.*

nyone who has a parent or grandparent born in the Republic of Ireland or Northern Ireland is eligible to receive an Irish passport. Acquiring this document will open the European Union to you, as well as offer advantages of a citizen. You can live, work, study, and retire in Ireland and any of the member states of the European Union, you can start your own business and take advantage of international tax treaties, you can travel overseas on a "neutral" Irish passport, and you never have to worry about obtaining work permits. Plus, you'll honor your heritage.

Contact the Chicago Irish Consulate for information regarding Irish Citizenship. They will mail the FBR/Irish Citizenship application forms to you, or you can obtain them online. If you have already gathered all the necessary official documents to prove your Irish lineage to a parent or grandparent, then carefully fill out the paperwork and return to the consulate for their approval.

If you're reading and hearing about this for the first time, read on to see if you qualify for Irish citizenship. If you do, then your next step is to find all the documents necessary to prove your relationship to an Irish born parent or grandparent. You need only to identify one parent or grandparent to qualify.

The following information is *from* the Chicago Irish Immigrant Support Web site, WWW.CI-IS.COM.

Irish Citizenship

Citizenship by Birth

• Anyone born in Ireland is an Irish citizen, except children of parents holding diplomatic immunity in Ireland.

• Anyone born outside Ireland, whose father or mother was born in Ireland, is an Irish citizen.

• If one of the above does not apply, citizenship is not automatic and must be acquired through application.

1892 Declaration for United States Citizenship.

Citizenship by Application

• Anyone born outside of Ireland, whose father or mother is an Irish citizen not born in Ireland, can become an Irish citizen by having his or her birth entered in the Irish Register of Foreign Births at the Department of Foreign Affairs in Dublin or at Chicago's Irish Consulate.

Irish Citizenship by Descent: Foreign Birth Registry (FBR)

If you have one Irish-born grandparent, then you qualify to apply for Irish citizenship through FBR. (There are certain limited circumstances where you may be eligible to obtain Irish citizenship through your great-grandmother or great-grandfather. This can be a bit complicated, but if your great-grandparent was born in Ireland and your parent used that relationship to register as an Irish Citizen by Descent by the time of your birth (not after), then you are also eligible for Irish citizenship. This is not automatic and must be acquired through application.)

To apply for your FBR you will need:

Documents Relating to Your Grandparent

• The full long form Irish birth certificate. Birth records have been maintained in Ireland since 1864 and certified copies may be obtained by contacting General Register Office, Convent Road, Roscommon, County Roscommon, Ireland, FAX: 011-353-90-6632999, Call 011-353-90-6632900, WWW.GROIRELAND.IE, click on Research. Requests should detail the grandparent's full name, and date and place of birth. If not known, this information might be found on death/marriage certificates. If you're planning a trip to Ireland and wish to search for these documents yourself, go to the General Register Office, Joyce House, Lombard Street East, Dublin, WWW.GROIRELAND.IE. Do not send mail requests to the Dublin office, it is for walk ins, only.

• The marriage certificate

• If the grandparent is deceased, the death certificate; if living, a current official photo I.D.

Documents Relating to Your Parent

• The full, long form, birth certificate of the parent related to the grandparent.

Their birth certificates must contain sufficient information in order to establish a clear relationship to the Irish-born grandparent.

• The marriage certificate

• If the parent is deceased, the death certificate; if living, a current official photo I.D.

Documents Relating to You the Applicant

• The full, long form birth certificate containing sufficient information to establish a clear relationship to the parent.

• Where there is a change of name, i.e. on marriage, supporting documentation must be provided, i.e. marriage license.

• Two recent passport type photos signed and dated on the back by a witness as indicated on the application form.

• Notarized copy of current US passport.

• Notarized copies of three additional proofs of identity, one of which must be a photo I.D. Provide a copy of bank statement/utility bill, showing your present address.

• In the case of a person under 18, the person submitting the application (parent or guardian) must also submit proofs of identity.

Important Note: Church certified baptismal and marriage certificates may be considered when an applicant can produce a statement from the relevant state authority to the effect that they have been unsuccessful in their search for the civil record.

Hospital certified birth certificates are not acceptable.

All official documents: birth, death, and marriage certificates: must be original or official copies from the issuing authority, properly sealed and stamped.

All of the above documents must have complete details that prove the connection. In other words, the birth certificate must show the names, dates of birth and places of birth of both your parents, so that they can be conclusively identified to be the same person mentioned on the marriage license and their own birth certificate. All the documents must be official, i.e., must bear the raised stamp of the issuing agency.

Important Web Sites:

The rules are specified in the Irish Nationality and Citizenship Act. Google: Irish Nationality and Citizenship Act.

Visit Chicago's Irish Immigrant Support Web site, WWW.CI-IS.COM, for additional information.

For information on visas, passports, and citizenship, visit HTTP://WWW.IRELANDMB.ORG.

Genealogy: The Search!

If you've been wondering about your Irish ancestry, then maybe it's time to figure it out. It's not enough that you've heard family stories about an Irishman somewhere in the mix; you'll want proof of kinship, especially if you're thinking of becoming an Irish citizen through Foreign Birth Registry. (Remember: you're eligible if one grandparent was born in Ireland.)

For those fortunate enough to know where in Ireland their ancestors emigrated from, you're ahead of the game. But don't get too cocky; unless you have documents to prove it, you're at square one.

Locating paperwork can be tricky. It helps to know names, dates of birth and death, and maiden names of ancestors who emigrated, and it's even better if a family member saved old documents. Ask relatives what they know and what they remember about an Irish connection. Search old trunks and papers, look for family bibles, and gather pictures. With a bit of diligence, you can collect enough information to get started on the genealogy trail.

I've taken the liberty of simplifying a rather complicated task in order to present this in a user-friendly manner. Set aside time each day or plan a few hours a week for recording, documenting and planning. Take one small step at a time. Each facility listed will provide assistance and good advice. I began my journey in much this same way, gathering documents from various Chicago sources and mulling over miles of microfilm until I was finally able to tap sources in Ireland. I had no idea which counties my four grandparents had emigrated from, nor did I know the years. My search yielded great success, and I even published a book detailing the journey.

You're not in this alone; there are lots of good sources and knowledgeable folks out there who are involved in their own searches. Many libraries offer assistance to those searching for information. So sharpen your pencils, pack your briefcase, and enjoy the journey to find your Chicago Irish.

Getting Started: The Four Ws

Begin by asking yourself the four Ws—who, why, when, and where.

Who: Determine the Irish surname or surnames you'll be researching. Don't rely on the spelling, because many names were altered. Folks who either couldn't understand the Irish accent or didn't care to ask the spelling incorrectly copied ship records. Some of your ancestors might even have voluntarily changed their names. Whatever the reason, figure out all the ways in which the surname could be spelled. Write them down and keep them handy. When seeking documents, you just might discover a different spelling along the way.

Why: Did they emigrate before or after the Great Famine? Did the landlords force them to leave or did they come on their own? Were they part of the wave of immigrants arriving in America in the early 1900s?

The 1830s saw a significant rise in immigration as conditions in Ireland continued to deteriorate. The Great Famine of 1845–1850 caused large numbers of Irish to leave their homeland. The potato blight, much like an earthquake or flood, was a natural disaster; but the British response was indifferent and completely devoid of common sense or compassion. No one accused the English of causing the potato to rot, but the English government was guilty of the criminal neglect of millions of starving people. Study your Irish history; you'll better understand their reasons for leaving..

When: If your ancestors arrived after 1892, the search will be a bit easier. Ellis Island was one of the more popular ports of entry and a good source of information. Before that time it was Castle Gardens in New York, along with other ports of entry such as Baltimore, Boston, New Orleans, and Philadelphia. Ellis Island records have been well preserved, are easy to read, and provide detailed information. You'll discover who sponsored your ancestors in America, how much money they arrived with, their eye color, their height, and if they traveled with relatives. If they entered via Canada and then made their way to the United States, you'll want to check Canadian immigration records.

Where: This is the larger question. Where did they live in Ireland? Where did they settle in America? This is where the relatives come in. Ask! Ask! Ask! Visit your oldest relatives and involve them in your search. Check attics, closets, and trunks for family bibles, old letters, news articles, and land deeds. Look through old photo albums together and have them identify persons, events, etc. Record what they tell you. Ireland might be a small island, but there are 32 counties and thousands of townlands and parishes. You'll need detailed information if you ever plan to locate the old cottages in Ireland.

Organization will be the key to your success. Find a space where you can gather, stack, and store documents. Think about ways in which you can file your information, and have a dedicated computer or computer folder for your use only. Purchase notebooks, pens, pencils, and erasers. Invest in a good laser printer, empty an old file cabinet and claim it as yours, and buy assorted plastic bins to create plenty of storage. The amount of paperwork you'll collect can be overwhelming, so make sure you file everything that comes in.

Collecting Paperwork

Begin with yourself and work backwards. Collect your marriage (if applicable), baptism, and birth certificates. Now gather the like certificates from the parent (either one or both) you are researching (Irish side). Include their death certificates, if applicable.

Once you've successfully located these documents, then begin to collect the paperwork on your Irish grandparents. Their marriage certificate might indicate that they were born in Ireland. If you find this to be the case, then you are eligible to receive your Irish citizenship, but you'll need the Irish birth certificate in order to qualify.

Each thread of information must be proven. Don't rely on hearsay or family legend. We would all like to believe we are descended from a great Irish hero or that our people owned large estates in Ireland before the British occupation, but that's unlikely. So put those stories aside and work only with what you know.

Records You'll Search in Chicago:

Birth certificates
Church/school records
Ship Passenger records
Baptismal certificates
Orphanage records
Social Security Death Index
Marriage certificates
Census records
Military records
Death certificates
Naturalization records
City directories
Cemetery records
Deeds
Newspapers
Wills

Where Do I Find Family Documents?:

You were bound to ask this question because most families don't keep records of past family members, so it's time to secure documents from other sources in Chicago. If you are unfamiliar with the records listed above, you can Google each subject for information. There's lots of knowledgeable experts out there willing to lend a hand, so don't hesitate to ask.

Birth, Marriage, and Death Records

Cook County Clerk's Office

Bureau of Vital Statistics
Cook County Building
118 North Clark Street
312/603-7790
www.cookctyclerk.com

Visit their Web site and print the necessary forms. The city of Chicago will release the following genealogy records: Birth records from the past 75 years, death records from the past 20 years, and marriage records from the past 50 years. If you can't complete all the information required on the forms, then you'll have to locate a source for that information. You might want to look for gravestone inscriptions; these will often provide the estimated age, which in turn will give you an idea of the date of birth. Sometimes they'll even list the name and place of birth. You might want to search old newspapers to check notices of births, marriages and deaths, as well as the obituaries. If you don't have exact dates, ask the Clerk's Office to search within a 5 or 10 year span. There may be an additional charge for this service, but it's well worth it. If this doesn't get it, then check out the U.S. Census, available from the Newberry Library, Family History Center and National Archives (information to follow.)

Illinois Regional Archives Depository (IRAD)

One University Plaza
MS BRK 140
Springfield
217/785-1266
www.cyberdriveillinois.com/departments/
archives/archives.html

Operates in tandem with the Abraham Lincoln Presidential Library and has seven centers in Illinois, all of which are located at Illinois state universities. They also store land deeds, mortgage records, tax records, voter registers, naturalization records including declaration of intent, probate records, coroner's inquest records, and jail registers.

Church, School, and Orphanage Records

Archdiocese of Chicago

Archives and Records Center
711 West Monroe Street
312/831-0711
jtreanor@archchicago.org

If you know the church that your ancestors attended, then make an inquiry about their baptismal, marriage, and burial records. Research for genealogical purposes is confined to records dating before to December 31, 1915. Researchers are looking for their own records, the archives staff will search any time period. Pre-1916 records are available for research on microfilm. Only records of closed parishes (complete list available upon request) are held by the archives. All open parishes keep their own records. The only exceptions to this are Old St. Mary's and St. Elizabeth's, whose earliest books are now at the archives.

Access to orphanage records is restricted. Only the person included in the record can request and receive information from his or her records. They also have records for approximately 250 closed Catholic schools in the Archdiocese. Access to these records is restricted to those mentioned in them. The archives also maintain collections of school yearbooks, class photographs, parish annual reports, and cemetery records.

Ship Records

Ellis Island
www.ellisisland.org

Ellis Island opened its doors to immigrants in 1892. Before that time, the majority of immigrants were being processed at Castle Gardens, New York. If your ancestors immigrated before the year 1892, it is safe to assume they entered through Castle Gardens; although, it was unusual for entry ports along the coast of the Atlantic to receive ship loads of immigrants. Records for Castle Gardens are sketchy but can be found.

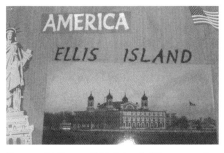

Statue of Liberty, Ellis Island. (Courtesy of Ellis Island.)

Castle Gardens
New York
www.castlegarden.org

America's first official immigration center, 1830 to 1892.

Immigrant Ships Transcribers Guild
www.immigrantships.net

Volunteers transcribe passenger lists from a variety of ports—if you don't have luck with Ellis Island or Castle Gardens.

The Ships List
www.theshiplist.com

Excellent place to find immigrant arrivals.

Census, Military, Ship, and Naturalization Records

National Archives and Records Administration
Great Lakes Region
7358 South Pulaski Road
773/948-9000
chicago.archives@nara.gov,
www.archives.gov/great-lakes/

The Archives has the 1790–1870 census schedules, a microfilm copy of the 1880 schedules, the surviving fragments of the 1890 schedules, and a microfilm copy of the 1900 and 1910 schedules; some military service and pension records; selected passenger ship records, and indexes for vessels arriving at New York and other U.S. ports; naturalization index covering parts of Illinois, Indiana, Iowa and Wisconsin. Available records span the period from 1790 to 1950. The self-service microfilm reading room operates on a reservation system. Researchers should call to reserve a microfilm reader. They do not accept e-mail reservations. Call 773/948-9020 to reserve a spot.

City Directories and Newspapers

Chicago History Museum
1601 North Clark Street
312/642-4600
www.chicagohs.org

They house a complete collection of Chicago city and telephone directories, dating from 1839 to present, as well as suburban directories for 1920–1971 as well as scattered holdings between 1978 and 1996. You'll find an extensive collection of Chicago newspapers. Search their online collection catalog for specific holdings.

You might be interested in their Address Conversion Guides. When doing research on past addresses, you'll need to know that in 1909 part of the Chicago street numbering system was altered. In addition, many Chicago street names have been changed. Guides to street numbering and street name changes are available in their research center.

Divorce, Probate, and Other Court Records

Circuit Court of Cook County

50 West Washington Street, Room 1113
312/603-6601
www.cookcountyclerkofcourt.org

Cemetery Records

Catholic Cemeteries of Chicago

708/449-6100
www.cathcemchgo.org

Here you will find a listing of all the Catholic cemeteries in the area. There is no central repository for Chicago-area cemetery records. You will need to contact the individual cemeteries for their records.

Other Cemeteries in Chicagoland

www.chicagolandyp.com

Enter the word *cemeteries* in keyword search.

Libraries and Other Resources

Family History Library

15 South Temple Street,
Salt Lake City, Utah
800/346-6004
www.familysearch.org

This is THE place for genealogists. An entire floor is dedicated to Irish/British records. You can find most everything that you'll need under one roof. If you're not able to travel to Salt Lake City, feel free to visit any of their kiosks in Chicago and suburbs to access their microfilm. Call to make an appointment at the following kiosks, as their hours of operation are limited:

Hyde Park, 5200 South University Avenue, 773/493-1830

Chicago Heights, 402 Longwood Drive, 708/756-1280

Buffalo Grove, 15 Port Clinton Road, 847/913-5387

Schaumburg, 130 West Schaumburg Road, 847/885-4130

Naperville, 1320 Ridgeland Avenue, 630/505-0233

Wilmette, 2801 Lake Avenue, 847/251-9818

You can also access these records at The Newberry Library in Chicago and the Arlington Heights Library in Arlington Heights, IL.

The Newberry Library

60 West Walton Street

312/943-9090

www.newberry.org

An amazing source for documents, the Newberry Library is an independent research facility devoted heavily to genealogical services; librarians with extensive experience in the field of genealogy staff the Newberry. Their collection strengths include family histories, local histories for counties and cities nationwide, city directories, biographical resources, vital record indexes, censuses, military records and histories, land ownership maps, and immigration information. They have available electronic resources such as Ancestry.com, HeritageQuest Online, Proquest Historical Chicago Tribune, and New England Historic Genealogical Society Databases. Laptops are permitted in reading rooms.

You can also access the Mormon's Family History Library in Salt Lake City, Utah, at the Newberry. The Family History Center is one of the premier genealogy resources in the country. Almost every document can be found here (including some—though not all—Irish birth certificates and baptism records, along with the Irish 1901 Census and Griffin's Valuation).

The Newberry Library also has a Quick Search service for those who are unable to travel to the Library or who would like someone to do a search for them. The staff will search a specific source and mail the results to you for a small fee. Visit Newberry's links at WWW.NEWBERRY.ORG/GENEALOGY

Public Libraries

Call your neighborhood branch. Many libraries have genealogy records and provide assistance. I found these libraries to be helpful:

Arlington Heights Public Library

500 North Dunton Avenue, Arlington Heights

847/392-0100

www.ahml.info.

This library is one of the designated branches of the Family History Center in Salt Lake City, Utah. You can access microfilm from their huge library containing Irish genealogy. One entire room is dedicated to genealogy. Contact Michael at 847/870-3643.

Beverly Branch of the Chicago Public Library

2121 West 95th Street

312/747-9673

www.chipublib.org/002branches/beverly

This collection is housed in the heart of the Beverly/Morgan Park community, home to a number of Irish American scholars and writers. Check out their array of Irish genealogy resources, along with Irish American newspapers, videos, phonodiscs, CDs, and audiocassettes. Visit their Web site for additional information.

Harold Washington Library

400 South State Street

www.chipublib.org

This main branch of the Chicago Public Library system has a good archive of newspapers.

Oak Lawn Public Library

9427 South Raymond Avenue, Oak Lawn

708/422-4990

www.lib.oak-lawn.il.us

Free access to the Social Security Death Benefits Index, Family History Network, Family TreeMaker, HeritageQuest, Cyndi's List, Canadian Genealogy, National Archives of Canada Genealogy Research, and Ontario Genealogy Society for those whose ancestors came through Canada into Chicago.

University of Illinois at Chicago

801 South Morgan Street

www.uic.edu/depts/lib

Not a municipal library, but available to the public, the UIC Library is a good source for old newspapers.

In Other Parts of Illinois

Abraham Lincoln Presidential Library

112 North Sixth Street, Springfield

217/558-8844

www.illinoishistory.gov/lib/default.htm

Illinois State Archives

Norton Building, Capitol Complex, Springfield

217/782-4682

www.sos.state.il.us/departments/archives/archives.htm

Publications

Family Chronicle

P.O. Box 194, Niagara Falls, New York 14304

www.familychronicle.com

Family Tree Magazine

P.O. Box 421385, Palm Coast, Florida 32142

www.familytreemagazine.com

Irish Roots Magazine

www.irishrootsmagazine.com

The Septs

**Irish Genealogy Society International,
5768 Olson Memorial Highway,
Golden Valley, Minnesota 55422
www.IrishGenealogy.org.**

Become a member and receive their quarterly journal. Volunteers staff their genealogy library. Irish researchers are available to assist you with your search.

Web Sites

Ancestors

www.pbs.org/kbyu/ancestors/charts.

Pedigree charts, family group sheets, research log, source notes, etc.

Ancestry.com

www.ancestry.com

The largest of all the commercial genealogy sties, they offer several subscription options, although some of the data is free.

Canadian Genealogy Centre

www.genealogy.gc.ca.

Passenger lists are coming aboard at this Canadian library and archives site. Good place to check for the emigrants who arrived in Canada before making their way to Chicago.

Chicago Genealogy

www.chicagogenealogy.com.

For local resources.

Cyndi's List

www.cyndislist.com.

A master list of genealogy sites.

Disney's Family Tree Maker

www.disney.go.com/disneyvideos/
animatefilms/tigermovie/familytree.html.

Fun for the kids and young at heart.

Roots Web

www.rootsweb.com

Another go-to site for all things related to ancestral research.

Resources in Ireland

When you begin your search in Ireland, if a name, place, or approximate date of birth, marriage, or death is known, the best point at which to begin is probably:

- **The Irish Census**, for a person living between 1901 and 1911.
- **Primary Valuation**, for a person living in the 1840s, 1850s, or 1860s.
- **Tithe Applotment Books**, for a person living in the 1820s or 1830s.

Church of Ireland Parish Records:
WWW.IRELAND.ANGLICAN/ORG/LIBRARY/
LIBRARY.HTML

Clare County Library Database:
WWW.CLARELIBRARY.IE

General Register Office:
WWW.GROIRELAND.IE

Land Registers of Northern Ireland:
WWW.NIRELAND.COM/GENEALOGY/
CONTACTS.HTML

Linen Hall Library: WWW.LINENHALL.COM

National Archives:
WWW.NATIONALARCHIVES.IE

National Library of Ireland: WWW.NLI.IE

Northern Ireland Resources—
Ulter-Irish: WWW.PRONI.NICS.GOV.UK

Public Library of Belfast:
WWW.BELB.ORG.UK

Public Libraries in Ireland:
WWW.LIBRARY.IE/PUBLIC

Valuation Office: WWW.VALOFF.IE

Genealogy by Genetics

Family Tree DNA

www.Irishroots.com

For information on family groups, contact:
MIKE@IRISHROOTS.COM

For all families of Irish decent who are interested in uncovering and identifying members of your family throughout the world. I'm sure you've wondered if your family descended from Vikings who settled in Ireland. What areas of Ireland or America might have family members that match your DNA? What name spellings show the exact same DNA matches? Which branch of the family tree do you spring from in Ireland? A DNA match may be able to help to answer some of these questions.

Family Tree DNA has pioneered the use of DNA testing in the field of genealogy, providing a new way to break through barriers in your family history. The genetic tests that they offer can determine relationships with a 99.9% degree of accuracy.

My family is in the O'Shea Project out of County Cork, Ireland. Our Project Administrator has informed us of three viable contacts. And as more Sheas join the project, the possibility of locating relatives increases. This is definitely the cutting edge of genealogy.

Most importantly, if you're wondering just how Irish you are, these results can provide a guide to the possibilities of where your ancestors came from. So check out the surname search to see if there's someone in Ireland gathering information on your family name.

Be sure to locate as much information as possible before heading off to Ireland. I suggest you have the following documents before booking your trip:

- Name of ancestor who left Ireland
- Approximate date of birth
- County and origin in Ireland
- Religious denomination
- Names of ancestor's parents
- Name of ancestor's spouse, date and place of marriage

Don't be discouraged! The time spent digging into old records and sleuthing around for clues will truly pay off, and you're sure to find information leading to your family. Remember that the journey may not an easy one, but the rewards are significant. You'll soon discover what has been a part of you since before you were born—that "Irish feeling," a feeling that will call you back to Ireland. Go n-éiri an bóthar leat! (Good journey!)

Recipes

rish cooking brings to mind good, hearty stew, boiled bacon and cabbage, and soda bread—stick-to-your-ribs kind of fare. It's always a treat to be invited to share delicious food cooked to perfection. But good cooking just got better, because I've kicked it up a notch by adding some of my favorite ingredients, Guinness and Irish whiskey, to a few of the recipes. The cakes are especially good when paired with a nice steaming pot of Irish tea.

Traditional soda bread does not contain yeast but instead consists of a combination of flour, buttermilk, and baking soda. I prefer adding a bit of sugar and egg for a sweeter taste. When baking the Whiskey Soda bread, soak the raisins in either Whiskey or tea, depending on your tastes. This creates a moist soda bread. And don't worry about the alcohol; it cooks away. Great flavor comes from adding the spirits. Beef Stew prepared with a bit of Guinness adds a unique flavor, and wait until you taste chicken marinated in this delicious stout. Enjoy these selections—my favorites!

Irish Breads and Cakes

Irish Soda Bread

4 cups all-purpose flour
4 tablespoons white sugar
1 teaspoon baking soda
1 tablespoon baking powder
½ teaspoon salt
½ cup margarine, softened
1 cup buttermilk
1 egg
¼ cup butter, melted
¼ cup buttermilk

Preheat oven to 375 degrees. Lightly grease a large baking sheet. In large bowl, mix together flour, sugar, baking soda, baking powder, salt, and margarine. Stir in 1 cup of buttermilk and egg. Turn dough onto a lightly floured surface and knead slightly. Form dough into a round and place on baking sheet. In small bowl, combine melted butter with ¼ cup buttermilk; brush loaf with this mixture. Cut an "X" into the top of loaf. Bake for 45 to 50 minutes or until inserted toothpick comes out clean.

Whiskey Soda Bread

1 cup raisins
½ cup Irish whiskey or tea
3 cups all-purpose flour
½ cup sugar
1 tablespoon baking powder
1 teaspoon salt
½ teaspoon baking soda

1⅓ cup buttermilk

¼ cup butter, melted

Soak raisins overnight in Irish whiskey or tea, if you prefer. Combine dry ingredients except soda. Mix well. Stir in raisins, mixing well. Dissolve soda in buttermilk, add flour mixture, stir in butter, and mix well. Spoon batter into a greased 2-quart casserole. Bake at 350 degrees for 50 minutes or until golden brown.

Irish Whiskey Brack

2 cups raisins

1 cup brown sugar

½ teaspoon cinnamon

¼ teaspoon nutmeg

4 tablespoons Irish whiskey

1¼ cup of tea

2 cups self-rising flour

2 eggs

Soak raisins along with brown sugar, cinnamon and nutmeg in the whiskey and tea overnight. Stir in flour and eggs and mix well. Pour into greased 8 inch round tin. Bake at 325 degrees for about 1½ hours.

Brown Soda Bread

1 cup white flour

3 cups whole-wheat flour

1½ teaspoon baking soda

1¼ teaspoon salt

1¼ cups buttermilk

Mix dry ingredients. Add buttermilk to make a soft dough. Turn onto a board and knead lightly. Make into a round, prick with a fork. Bake at 400 degrees for 35 minutes.

Irish Pound Cake

1 cup of butter

1 cup of sugar

1 cup of flour

4 large eggs

¼ teaspoon of grated lemon rind

¼ teaspoon baking powder

2 cups of raisins

2 tablespoons Irish whiskey

Mix egg and sugar, add lemon rind, add eggs, and mix well. Add all flour, baking powder and raisins. Mix well. Pour in greased cake pan. Bake at 350 degrees for 45 minutes or longer, and watch for top to brown. Remove from oven and pour whiskey over the cake.

Guinness Cake

½ cup butter

1 cup brown sugar

3 eggs

2¼ cup flour

½ teaspoon cinnamon

Pinch of salt

½ cup raisins, soaked in Guinness for 24 hours

1⅓ cup golden raisins: soaked

¼ cup dried cherries

8 ounces Guinness

Heat oven to 350 degrees. Cream butter, sugar, and eggs. Mix together flour, salt, cinnamon, and soaked raisins and cherries. Mix in the Guinness. Grease 8-inch cake pan. Bake for two hours or until firm in the center.

Irish Meat and Potatoes

Traditional Boxty

½ lb raw potato

½ lb mashed potatoes

½ lb white flour

2 tablespoons milk

1 egg

Salt and pepper

Grate raw potatoes. Add your cooked mashed potatoes. Add salt, pepper, and flour. Beat eggs and add to mixture with just enough milk to make a dropping batter. Drop by teaspoonfuls onto a frying pan until browned.

Colcannon

4 pounds potatoes

1 pound cooked cabbage

1 ounce butter

½ pint milk

6 chopped onions (small)

Peel and boil potatoes. Drain and mash until smooth. Add onions to milk and bring to a boil. Add to potato and beat until fluffy. Beat in finely chopped cabbage and butter.

Corned Beef and Cabbage in Guinness

4 pounds corned beef

12 ounces Guinness

1 medium onion

3 cloves garlic

1 bay leaf

¼ teaspoon ground cinnamon

¼ teaspoon ground cloves

¼ teaspoon allspice

¼ teaspoon ground black pepper

1 head of cabbage, cut into wedges

6 medium white potatoes, peeled and quartered

1 pound carrots, peeled and cut into pieces

Brown corned beef on all sides over high heat. Pour Guinness over meat, add enough water to cover. Add onion, garlic, bay leaf, cinnamon, cloves, allspice, and pepper. Bring pot to a boil and skim off any foam. Reduce flame and simmer for three hours. Add carrots, potatoes and cabbage. Cover and continue cooking until meat and vegetables are tender (about 30 minutes).

Irish Beef Stew in Guinness

1 pound stew meat cut into small pieces

2 tablespoons olive oil

½ onion, diced

4 potatoes

4 carrots

2 cups beef broth

6 ounces Guinness

Brown meat and onion in olive oil. Add Guinness when the meat begins to brown. Stir well, making sure to scrape the bottom of the pan (that's what makes the good gravy). When the Guinness boils down, add the beef broth. Put to simmer and cover. When that liquid has boiled down, add either a bit more Guinness or beef broth, whichever you prefer. Simmer for about two hours. Stir every now and then. Add potatoes (cut into small pieces) and carrots. Simmer for another hour or so. Thicken gravy with a teaspoon of cornstarch. Delicious! The Guinness flavor makes this an exceptional stew.

Beef Pie with Guinness

1½ pounds ground meat

1 diced onion

1 garlic clove

2 tablespoons flour

6 ounces tomato sauce

½ teaspoon red wine vinegar

1 tablespoon Dijon mustard

Pinch of salt and freshly ground pepper

6 ounces Guinness

Pastry dough (found in the refrigerator aisle of your local market)

Brown ground meat and onions in olive oil. Add a clove of garlic. Stir in flour and tomato sauce. Add vinegar, mustard, salt, pepper, and Guinness. Stir well. Cover and let simmer for 20 minutes (if it's too soupy, let the liquid boil down to a meaty consistency). Roll out the pastry dough and put into pie dish. Add meat mixture, cover with piecrust, poke holes on top, glaze with egg white and water mixture. Bake at 425 degrees for 20 minutes or until the piecrust is golden. Serve with gravy.

Parsley Liquor Gravy

1 ounces butter

1 ounces cornstarch

10 ounces beef broth

4 tablespoons chopped fresh parsley

Salt and ground pepper

4 tablespoons Guinness

Stir all ingredients together, bringing to a boil. Keep a watch on this, stirring constantly, for it gets lumpy very quickly. When it reaches desired consistency, it's ready to serve.

Guinness BBQ Chicken

3 pounds cut up chicken

1 bottle Guinness

1 tablespoon dark brown sugar

1 tablespoon lemon juice

1 tablespoon vegetable oil

1 tablespoon dark molasses

Arrange chicken in 2-quart baking dish. Mix ingredients and pour over chicken. Refrigerate 6 hours or overnight, turning several times. Bake at 350 degrees for one hour.

More Ideas with Guinness

• Try baking your bratwurst in Guinness before grilling; the Guinness perks up the taste, and your family and friends will be clamoring for more.

• And add a bit of Guinness to your spaghetti sauce. While you're browning the meat, add the Guinness. When it boils down, add your tomatoes and sauce. It's delicious and good for you.

• Next time you're making gravy, pour in a bit of Guinness; the flavor is outstanding.

Irish Coffee

4 tablespoons Irish whiskey

1 teaspoon brown sugar

Freshly made coffee

Whipped cream

Pour whiskey into warmed glass. Stir in sugar. Pour in coffee. Add a dollop of whipped cream.

Bibliography

Books

Caherty, Mary. *Real Irish Cookery*. Great Britain: Robert Hale Limited, 1987.

Hayes, Tadhg. *Gift of the Gab*. Dublin: The O'Brien Press,1997.

Hayes, Tadhg. *The Wit of Irish Conversation*. Dublin: The O'Brien Press, 2004.

Coughlan, Gerry, and others. *Irish Language & Culture*. Australia: Lonely Planet Publications, 2007.

Nolan, Brendan. *The Irish Companion*. London: Thinking Publishing, 2006.

Newspaper Articles

Heist, Lauren, "Don't Mess with Perfection," *Daily Herald*, March 2007.

Lester, Kerry, "Get your Green On," *Daily Herald*, March 2007.

Magazine Articles

Mooney, John, "Profiling Boxing," *Irish American News*, April 2006.

O'Shaughnessy, Tamara, "Irish Immersion," *Chicago Parent Magazine*, Spring 2007.

Slack, Steve, "Smilin' Irish Eyes," *Midwest Living Magazine*, April 2007.

Internet

Bude, Christine, "St. Patrick's Day in the Chicago Area," WWW.ASSOCIATEDCONTENT.COM, 2007.

Budell, Karen, "Beverly Thrills," WWW.CHICAGO.METROMIX.COM, 2007.

Carey, Mairead, "Croke Park Open for Soccer," WWW.IRISHABROAD.COM, 2007.

Carter, Adam, "St. Patrick's Day in Chicago," WWW.THELOCALTOURIST.COM, 2007.

City of Chicago, "St. Patrick's Day-South Side Irish," WWW.PLANET99.COM, 2007.

Clark, Sandy, "Get Your Irish Up," WWW.FINDARTICLES.COM, 2007.

Demand Entertainment, "Speak with an Irish Accent," WWW.SOYOUWANNA.COM, 2007.

Dolan, Terence, "Vocabulary and Grammar of Hiberno-English," WWW.HIBERNO-ENGLISH.COM, 2005.

Editor, "Guinness Oyster Festival," WWW.CHICAGOEVENTS.COM, 2007.

Editor, "Hot Boxing News," WWW.HOTBOXINGNEWS.COM, 2007.

Editor, "St. Patrick's Day Events," WWW.CHICAGOREADER.COM, 2007.

Editor, "Women's Boxing Network," WWW.HOTBOXINGNEWS.COM, 2007.

Emerson, Jim, "Drama of Irish Troubles," WWW.SUNTIMES.COM, 2007.

Gleiberman, Owen, "The Wind That Shakes the Barley," WWW.EW.COM, 2007.

Harron, Maurice, "Grainne," WWW.CHICAGOSISTERCITIES.COM, 2006.

Haymarket Group, "Pubs," WWW.CHICAGOIRISH.ORG, 2006.

Hundley, Tom, "Irish Language Comeback," WWW.CHICAGOTRIBUNE.COM, 2004.

Hopkins, Gary, "The Great Chicago Fire," WWW.EDUCATIONWORLD.COM, 2006.

Houllihan, Mike, "Where Good Times Are a Chief Concern," Chicago Sun Times site, WWW.SUNTIMES.COM, 2004

Irish Abroad, "Pubs," WWW.IRISHABROAD.COM/IRISHWORLD.COM, 2006.

Kelly, Aidan, "The Wearin' O' The Green," WWW.THECRIMSON.COM, 2007.

LaMorte, Chris, "Happy St. Fatty's Day," WWW.METROMIXCHICAGOTRIBUNE.COM, 2007.

Larson, Scott, "Real Ireland Please Stand," WWW.SCOTTSMOVIES.COM, 2006.

Metsch, Steve, "Tis the Season to be Irish," WWW.DAILYSOUTHTOWN.COM, 2007.

Moloney, Valerie, "Pints of View," WWW.CHICAGO.METROMIX.COM, 2006.

Oppenheimer, Jean, "Celtic Dawn," WWW.BOXOFFICE.COM, 1996.

Przecha, Donna, "They Changed Our Name at Ellis Island," WWW.GENEALOGY.COM, 2006.

Parnell, Sean, The Chicago Bar Project, WWW.CHICAGOBARPROJECT.COM, 2007.

Papazian, "Bagpipes," WWW.CRANFORDPUB.COM, 2005.

Powell, Kimberly, "Claiming Irish Citizenship," WWW.GENEALOGY.ABOUT.COM, 2002.

Quirk, Kathy, UWM Celtic Studies, WWW.4.UWM.EDU, 2006.

Sofo, Virginia, "Green Beer and St. Patrick's Day," WWW.CHICAGO.ABOUT.COM, 2007.

Stefanow, Meagan, "Bodhrán Drum," WWW.SMITH.EDU/HSC/MUSEUM, 1998.

Sterling Scott Publishing, "Getting An Irish Passport," WWW.IRELAND-FUN-FACTS.COM, 2006.

Sullivan, Rosemary, "No Girls Allowed," WWW.CHICAGOTRIBUNE.COM, 2007.

Thornton, Nancy, "St. James at Sag Bridge Church and Cemetery," WWW.CANALHERITAGE.COM, 2006.

Traudt, Claudia, "Bloomsday Yes," WWW.UCHIBLOGO.UCHICAGO.EDU, 2006.

CDs

Henry, Kevin. *One's Own Place—A Family Tradition*. Bogfire, Inc., 1998.

Various Artists. *Hidden Treasures: Irish Music in Chicago*. Big Chicago Records, 2000.

Other Sources

Chicago Gaelic Park Newsletters, Oak Forest, IL.

Chicago History Museum.

Irish American Newspaper, Oak Park, IL, 2007.

NARA, Chicago.

Newberry Library, Chicago.

The Heritage Line Newsletters, The Irish American Heritage Center, Chicago.

Index

About the Author

Sharon Shea Bossard is an Irish citizen who earned her master's degree in Education from Chicago's Northeastern Illinois University. Curious about her Irish family's experiences as struggling immigrants in Chicago, she meticulously recorded their lives. That venture took an interesting turn with the successful publication of her first book, *Finding My Irish*, where she not only reveals to her readers the difficulties and rewards of the search, but also tells the story of her grandparents' journey from rural County Roscommon to the modern city of Chicago in 1903. Earning excellent reviews in all major Irish and Irish American publications, her book has been featured on numerous radio and television talk shows in Ireland and the United States. Her writing has appeared in the *Irish Genealogical Society International* magazine, and she continues to address professional organizations throughout the country, inspiring others to embark on their own journey of discovery. Sharon is a member of Chicago's Irish American Heritage Center, Gaelic Park, County Roscommon Midwest Association, County Kerry Club of Chicago, Illinois Women's Press Association, and the Writer's Workshop in Barrington. Visit her Web site, WWW.FINDINGMYIRISH.COM.

Publisher's Credits

Cover design by Timothy Kocher. Interior design and layout by Todd Petersen. Editing by Diana Solomon. Proofreading by Sharon Woodhouse and Therese Newman. Index by Martin L. White. Cover photos of the Shannon Rovers, Chicago River, and Mayor Daley by Dean Battaglia.

Lake Claremont Press

Founded in 1994, Lake Claremont Press specializes in books on the Chicago area and its history, focusing on preserving the city's past, exploring its present environment, and cultivating a strong sense of place for the future. Visit us on the Web at WWW.LAKECLAREMONT.COM.

Selected Booklist

A Native's Guide to Chicago

Sports Traveler Chicago

Wrigley Field's Last World Series

Food, Lodging, Liquor: Signs You're In Chicago

Oldest Chicago

The Chicago River Architecture Tour

Today's Chicago Blues

Chicago TV Horror Movie Shows: From Shock Theatre to Svengoolie

The Golden Age of Chicago Children's Television

Great Chicago Fires

For Members Only: A History and Guide to Chicago's Oldest Private Clubs

I Am a Teamster: A Short, Fiery Story of Regina V. Polk, Her Hats, Her Pets, Sweet Love, and the Modern-Day Labor Movement

Rule 53: Capturing Hippies, Spies, Politicians, and Murderers in an American Courtroom

From Lumber Hookers to the Hooligan Fleet: A Treasury of Chicago Maritime History

Graveyards of Chicago

Award-winners

A Cook's Guide to Chicago

The Streets & San Man's Guide to Chicago Eats

A Chicago Tavern: A Goat, a Curse, and the American Dream

The Chicago River: A Natural and Unnatural History

The Politics of Place: A History of Zoning in Chicago

Finding Your Chicago Ancestors